Roger Mardis, a valued a  yet. His insights into the v his topographical knowle~~~ insight. Each page contains nuggets of gold in which you will benefit. I recommend *Peaks and Pits* without reservation.

Rob Jackson, Vice President
Volunteers of America SE

As chairman of the board for the Nazareth Baptist School (NBS), the only Evangelical Christian K–12 school in Israel that is recognized by the Ministry of Education, I want to thank Pastor Roger for bringing a clear focus to this land in his work *Peaks and Pits*. I hope you will read this book to get better acquainted with the Holy Land from a theoretical and historical angle and then come and visit us personally. We at NBS will welcome your visit. May God use *Peaks and Pits* to enrich your faith and grow your understanding of this amazing land.

Najed Azzam, Chairman of the Board
Nazareth Baptist School

I've known Roger Mardis for nearly fifty years. Throughout our lives, we've both experienced our share of highs and lows. Using biblical stories from the Holy Land's topography, this book will help you to better serve others during your peak moments and to draw close to our Lord during the pits.

Daughtry Perritt, Founder and CEO
Pet Depot, Inc.

Roger Mardis's newest book, *Peaks and Pits*, uses geographical highs and lows in the Holy Land to help readers discover their own spiritual peaks and pits. This resource will help one uncover nuggets about biblical locations while successfully correlating each to one's spiritual journey. The attached questions are a valuable tool.

Donna P. Chisam, Executive Director
Friends of Nazareth, Inc.

This is not only a good read but a good read with practical application. I'm sure you will enjoy *Peaks and Pits*, I sure did.

David Pierce, National Wealth Management Acquisition Specialist
CBSI, Inc.

This is another gift written by my friend, Dr. Roger Mardis. Roger has walked through the hills and valleys of this land and of life. This book offers us encouragement when we experience life's good and bad times. On every page, you will find opportunities to reflect, grow, and learn. You will enjoy this book, and your heart will be encouraged as you reflect on biblical passages and locations. There are lessons for every stage of life.

Dr. Sarah Mielke, Principal
Westminster Christian School, Louisiana

What a privilege to endorse both this book and its author. I have known Roger since he was a young boy, running through the hallways of my home church. Today, the student has long since become the teacher. This book is a history book of the Holy Land; it is a devotional book with deep spiritual insights. It could be a textbook in a seminary class. Reading *Peaks and Pits* will impact you in many ways; it is a treasure for anyone who wants to better understand the land that Jesus chose as His earthly homeland.

Ken Edmundson, Founder of the ShortTrack Management
System, CEO of the Edmundson Group, and author of
Short Track CEO and *Teamwork: A Corporate Guide*

Dr. Mardis and I have been friends for decades. We were actually seminary classmates. *Peaks and Pits* is a thrilling read, where history meets reality. I love the writing style and the stories. This book is written from the heart of a pastor who loves God's Word. These words will encourage readers and strengthen their soul. Don't just read this book; study it for your personal spiritual growth.

Representative C. Brandt Smith, Jr., PhD
Jonesboro, Arkansas

Roger and I have been friends for over forty years, and I have enjoyed watching God take and use his life for the Glory of the Kingdom. I love it when God places a call on a man's life and then you watch as God orchestrates his path. Roger is a man who has given his life for others, and he continues to do so with the Nazareth Baptist School. You will enjoy these pages. I sure did.

Rex Jones, President
Christian Community Foundation

The Christian life certainly has its ups and downs, its peaks and pits. However, we know that wherever our God takes us, He will be faithful and present, for He is the God of the hills and valleys (1 Kings 20:28). This latest book by my good friend Roger Mardis is sure to encourage and equip you in both your highs and lows of life.

Scott Price, Senior Pastor
Fellowship Chapel, Bristol, VA

Breaking pita bread over an open fire in Nazareth, I was blown away by the depth of Roger's devotion to the land of the Bible. His fingerprints cover mission projects across the city of Nazareth, the hometown of our Lord Jesus. Of the hundreds of devotionals I have read, this is one book that stands unique, as it journeys the reader through the real world of the Bible. We not only read Scripture; we are immersed in it as we see the culture and customs that surround the biblical narrative of history. Roger brings it all to life. The title alone tells me to "Put on your sandals and get ready for a wild adventure." The peaks and pits of modern life are paralleled in these pages and the author takes us through with hope and confidence. Thank you, Roger, for being a key part of the first Student Leadership Nazareth. Your willingness to reach students in the land is a great gift.

Jay Strack, President
Student Leadership University

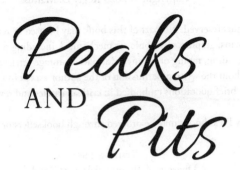

Peaks AND Pits

How the Land of the Bible Reflects the Life of a Believer

ROGER D. MARDIS

Foreword by Governor Mike Huckabee

WESTBOW
PRESS®
A DIVISION OF THOMAS NELSON
& ZONDERVAN

WestBow Press books may be ordered through booksellers or by contacting:

WestBow Press
A Division of Thomas Nelson & Zondervan
1663 Liberty Drive
Bloomington, IN 47403
www.westbowpress.com
844-714-3454

Scripture taken from the NEW AMERICAN STANDARD BIBLE®,
Copyright © 1960,1962,1963,1968,1971,1972,1973,1975,1977,1995 by
The Lockman Foundation. Used by permission. www.Lockman.org

ISBN: 978-1-6642-0923-7 (sc)
ISBN: 978-1-6642-0924-4 (hc)
ISBN: 978-1-6642-0922-0 (e)

Library of Congress Control Number: 2020920294

Print information available on the last page.

WestBow Press rev. date: 11/25/2020

It is my joy and honor to dedicate this book to the memory of my dad, William B. (Bill) Mardis (1936-2014), and my father-in-law, Billy Max Stephens (1943-2012). Michelle and I were both blessed with great dads who were great men and who made a great impact on us and so many others.

"Be on the alert, stand firm in the faith, act like men, be strong. Let all you do be done in love" (1 Corinthians 16:13–14).

Contents

Foreword

As you may know, I too have a deep love for the land of Israel and have been there many times. In fact, I have actually visited each of the locations spoken of in this book. I can honestly attest that the Holy Land is not only a land of milk and honey; it is a terrain of hills and valleys.

In addition to the land being like that, so are our lives: mine, yours, everyone's. I have personally enjoyed some great accomplishments and have experienced what many would call successes or mountains. I have also had my share of defeats, criticisms, and hardships. Yes, even governors go through valleys. I have known some peaks and pits.

In *Peaks and Pits*, Dr. Mardis, a seasoned pastor, reminds us how the ups and downs in Israel can reflect the highs and lows in life. In other words, we can learn about our Lord and our life by seeing them through the topography of this land.

Having pastored for many years myself, and having studied the Bible for decades, I have come to value a good resource that is theologically pure, devotionally appealing, and practically helpful. The book you hold in your hand is that type of resource. The thirty chapters before you will take you to thirty locations and will contain thirty lessons. No, there are really many more lessons than that.

Whether it is in your personal devotion time, in a small group setting, or in another congregational format, *Peaks and Pits* is a great read and a valuable resource. I encourage you to get your copy today; I am glad I got mine.

Governor Mike Huckabee

Preface

As a pastor and a student, I've had the opportunity to read my fair share of books, sit through hours of meetings, and attend hundreds of classes and conferences. During that period of time, I've written down many notes, quotes, and pithy statements. Perhaps it was a sermon outline or an effective illustration. Never did it cross my mind to document all the sources or settings so I wouldn't later be accused of plagiarizing someone else's idea.

I don't pretend that all the material in this book is original with me. Yes, I did write it all, but no, I didn't think it all up. What I did was gather a lot of bullets, and if they fit my gun, well, I fired away. As one preacher said years ago, "I've milked from many cows but made my own butter."

The goal of this book is not to offer original ideas or display scholarly thought; rather, it is to encourage other believers who might be enjoying a mountain or enduring a valley. Whether it's a peak or a pit, these pages have a challenge for you. I hope you will enjoy.

Remember, there is joy in the journey.

An Aid for Your Exploration

N
W —⟨✦⟩— E
S

At the conclusion of each day's reading, there are a few questions you can read and study through that will make your journey, whether it's scaling the peaks of a mountain or descending into the depths and darkness of a valley, a little bit more navigable and meaningful.

These questions are intended to stir up thought or discussion. Your small group or Bible study class can use this tool to heighten interaction. The list of questions is not long, and it certainly is not exhaustive; many others can be added.

I do hope you'll utilize these tools to better help you understand the pits and appreciate the peaks.

Acknowledgments

This book, like so many others, is not merely the work of a single writer. Many people have contributed in many ways to enable *Peaks and Pits* to become a reality. I sure hope to not leave anyone out, but I do want to thank the following for their help and efforts:

- Cyndi Rogers has been a faithful friend and ministry partner for years. Last year, she began working in our Friends of Nazareth (FON) office. She can interpret my handwriting, read my mind, and convey my thoughts (kind of scary). Thanks, Cyndi.
- Highland Baptist Church in Florence, Alabama is where our office is located; they have been gracious hosts.
- Many people proofed and corrected this work before publication. To each of you, thanks.
- Much appreciation to Steve Cox for his friendship and support of this project; blessings, my friend.
- To all my team at WestBow Publishers, thank you for your help and support.
- Thank you, Clayton, for some great photographs and for your friendship.
- Amer Nicola is not only a great guide in the Holy Land, he has become a dear friend, and he is a faithful Christ follower. He has taken me to most of the places in this book. Thanks, Amer.

- To my awesome wife, Michelle, thank you for your patience and encouragement as I've finished this project. You truly make the journey enjoyable.
- Last but not least, this book has been written for the glory and honor of Jesus Christ alone and to advance His cause in His hometown. *Soli Deo Gloria.*

Roger D. Mardis, President
Friends of Nazareth
Florence, Alabama
rogermardis.com

Introduction

For the Lord your God is bringing you into a good land ... flowing forth in valleys and hills. (Deuteronomy 8:7)

But the land into which you are about to cross to possess it (is) a land of hills and valleys. (Deuteronomy 11:11)

Valleys and hills, hills and valleys; such is the topography of the Holy Land, the land of Israel. It doesn't matter your location or vantage point. From the mountain peaks in the North, along the Lebanon and Syria borders, one can look out across the land to other high places and just as many valleys. Along the coastal plain near the beautiful Mediterranean Sea, one can view mountains on the horizon. Jerusalem is surrounded by mountains. The Dead Sea, the lowest place on the earth, is bordered by mountains such as Mount Nebo and Masada. Likewise, the Sea of Galilee is attached to the Golan Heights, the Valley of Doves, and Mount Arbel.

One of the great joys of my life has been to make many journeys to the Holy Land. When I begin to train a group of people for an upcoming trip, I always remind them that they need to be in good spiritual and physical shape. Groups will be walking, climbing, descending, and then some. You may walk as many as twenty thousand steps per day, and none of those are flat.

Why? Because this very special piece of land is not just holy, it is hilly.

Hills and valleys not only describe the land of Israel; it also describes life.

Everyone will have times in their life when they will scale the mountain peaks of success or find themselves enjoying the benefits of a great family, education, or career. However, life and history tell us that these same people will face their share of dark and difficult valleys. All it takes is a phone call, a diagnosis, a pink slip, or divorce papers. In those moments, it may not matter where you work or how much you know.

At one season in my life, I thought I would have a career in coaching. Not that I was ever a good athlete, but I always loved the game and athletics. I still enjoy watching way too many games.

As I was preparing this manuscript, news broke that Lane Kiffin had been hired as the University of Mississippi's new head football coach. I've been well aware of Kiffin's amazing and agonizing career (especially when he moved to Alabama and worked with Nick Saban).

Kiffin talks about his mountains. He has coached three Heisman Trophy winners, won two National Championships, been the youngest head coach in the National Football League, and earned million-dollar contracts and long winning streaks. He also recalls the valleys: He was fired midway through his second season with the Oakland Raiders; there were campus riots when he left the University of Tennessee; and he was fired at USC. His is a life of highs and lows, positives and negatives, good times and bad.

Coach Kiffin is a work in progress.

So am I.

So are you.

The Christian life is similar to the Holy Land. There will be some mountains, and there will be some valleys. The truth is, you probably won't stay on either for long.

For almost six decades, I have been learning about life, and in the last few years (since 2014), I have taken an interest in the Holy Land. In these pages, I will try to whet your appetite concerning Israel and at the same time try to help us all get a better handle on this thing called life. Like Moses and Peter and Coach Kiffin, I too have enjoyed some victories (mountains) and struggled through some valleys.

I hope you will join with me and glean what we can from Israel's, and life's, peaks and pits.

Valley of Shinar

Genesis 11

When you first saw the name Shinar, you probably wondered, *Where in the world is that?* Or maybe you thought, *I've never heard of that one.* But really you have, though maybe by another name. Shinar is the geographical location for the city of Babel, in which Nimrod and a host of others built a tower, the Tower of Babel. Oh, that Shinar!

The Valley (or plains) of Shinar is located between the Tigris and Euphrates Rivers in southern Mesopotamia or south Babylon(ia). This area is to the north of the Persian Gulf.

Many historians and theologians suggest that the events of Genesis 11 actually occur prior to those of chapter 10, and the "scattering" of chapter 10 is a result of the judgment of God on their rebellious actions. Perhaps it is placed here to smoothly lead into the genealogy of Shem and our introduction to Abraham. As such, the intent is not to be chronological but literary.

The Tower of Babel story is one of the four key events in Genesis 1–11. In each of the four areas—Creation, Fall, Flood, Babel (nations)—humanity disobeys God, the Lord judges sin, and in grace, God provides a fresh start. It really is true; the common thread and underlying theme of the entire Bible is one of grace and redemption.

Babel, in the village of Shinar, is more than just a geographical location. It is a psychological rallying point, a place where people could say, "Look what we've done." Humankind has always wanted its own utopia or society apart from God, or one in which God is excluded or not wanted. Kind of reminds me of much of our society today. It's the kind of place where you worship the creature or creation but not the Creator.

Dr. Henry M. Morris, in the *Biblical Basis for Modern Science,* suggests that after the Flood, the seventy family groups named would represent about a thousand people. Geometric progressions are slow to build at first. So it is very much possible for "the whole earth" to gather in this valley. Don't forget: God had told Noah's descendants after the Flood "to be fruitful and multiply, and fill the earth" (Genesis 8:17; 9:1, 7). It wasn't God's plan for them to "settle in Shinar."

Look at what happened. They began to "make bricks" (when God builds, He uses stones), and their intention was to build a tower (ziggurat) that would "reach into the heavens." People wanted to build a city, a tower, and a name for themselves. Three times, man said, "Let us." When humanity utters, "Let us go up," God responds, "Come, let Us go down" (Genesis 9:7). This interaction reminds me of Proverbs 19:21: "Many plans are in a man's heart, But the counsel of the Lord will stand." Or Psalm 2:4: "He who sits in the heavens laughs, the Lord scoffs at them."

Humankind wanted its tower to reach into the heavens. This project would look similar to a pyramid, but with each level recessed. This way, it was like a stairway to heaven. At the top would have been a shrine or altar in which sacrifices could be made. Several of these towers have been excavated in recent years.

Let us build a city.
Let us build a tower.
Let us build for ourselves a name.

Really, the underlying issue in Shinar was pride, and when it surfaces, "God will bust your Babel." I once heard Pastor Scott Price say that, and I've never forgotten it.

Babel was humans once again listening to the enemy, who had said to Adam and Eve, "You can be like God" (Genesis 3:5). Pride has its origin in the attitude and actions of Lucifer, who wanted his own throne in heaven and sought worship for himself. So let's develop this issue of pride.

The Person of Pride (Isaiah 14; Ezekiel 28)

Isaiah 14 and Ezekiel 28 are two passages in the Bible that speak of the origin of the devil and of evil. These texts are believed to depict a mighty monarch whose pride led to his destruction. This happens to the King of Tyre and to Belshazzar, but the prophets saw in these events something far deeper. In the fall of the kings of Tyre and Babylon, they saw the defeat of Satan, the prince of the world.

Lucifer was the highest of God's angels. He tried to usurp the throne of God and occupy it himself. Think of what Ezekiel says of Satan: He was the wisest creature (28:12), created in beauty (28:12b), protected the throne of God (28:14), and he was blameless (28:15). Though Ezekiel doesn't tell us, Isaiah tells us the thing that brought Satan down was pride. He wasn't fulfilled in just protecting the throne; he wanted to occupy it. And God had to "burst his Babel."

Truth: If pride can make a devil out of an angel, it can make a mess out of humankind.

The Pursuit of Pride (Genesis 3:1–5)

Once fallen from heaven, the enemy crawled his way back into the pages of scripture in the book of Genesis, in the garden of Eden, and at Shinar. Just like he told Eve in the garden, he convinced Nimrod and others in Babylonia that you don't need God's Word, you don't have to conform to God's ways, and you don't need to obey God's commands. Make it about yourself—I, me, my, mine. Pride will get you every time.

Truth: Pride makes us feel we don't need God, His love, His salvation, or His ways.

The Problems with Pride (Genesis 11:1–9)

The events in the Valley of Shinar illustrate well what pride can do in your life. In fact, it is pride that is at the center of every sin we commit, and it is our pride that causes God to say, "Let us go down."

- Pride will destroy you: "Pride goes before destruction" (Proverbs 16:18).
- Pride creates strife and friction: "Through pride comes nothing but strife" (Proverbs 13:10).
- Pride will create a downfall: "A man's pride will bring him low" (Proverbs 29:23).
- Pride will result in condemnation: "And not a new convert so he won't become prideful and fall into condemnation incurred by the devil" (1 Timothy 3:6).
- Pride defiles a person: "Pride, these things proceed from the heart of man and defile him" (Mark 7:22–23).

It is said of pride, "it is the only disease known to man that makes everyone sick but the one who has it."

Truth: Pride is at the core of every sin we commit, and it will lead to our ultimate destruction.

The Path from Pride (Philippians 2:1–8; James 4:5–10)

As we read these two passages, it is obvious that the pathway from pride is seen in following the person of humility—Jesus Christ. The antithesis of Lucifer is our Lord. If we are to combat and conquer pride, we will require a dynamic and personal relationship with the Lord.

Truth: We will overcome issues of pride only in our relationship with Christ, not in the "bricks" of a self-centered life.

I doubt any of my readers have ever attempted to build a tower reaching into the heavens, but there are times when we've all sought to build our lives our way, without consulting or obeying God. I'm guilty. You probably are as well. It will do us all good to stay away from Shinar.

Exploration Guide

W ⬥ E

N

S

1. What are the four key events in Genesis 1–11? How did God respond to each?
2. How would you define "pride"? Why is pride such a serious issue?
3. What are some of the ways the Bible describes Satan?
4. What are some characteristics of pride and of humility?
5. Go back and read the four "Truth" statements, and take some time to meditate on each. Discuss.

Mount Sodom, the Dead Sea

Genesis 13, 19

It may seem ironic that we can find a mountain on the lowest place on earth, but we can. It's more of a symbolic mound, but its story stands out in the biblical narrative and in the history of the Holy Land. We're talking about Sodom, as in Sodom and Gomorrah, and the mounds of destruction that her judgment left behind.

The Dead Sea and the region around it are actually beautiful sights to behold. The Dead Sea is situated some thirteen hundred feet below sea level; this mineral-rich body of water is located at the end of the Jordan River and serves as the southeast border of Canaan. There were several other names for this sea: Salt Sea, Sea of the Plain, Eastern Sea, and Sea of Arabah. It wasn't referred to as the Dead Sea until the second century.

It's amazing, but even though six million tons of water flows into this sea and it has no outlets, its level decreases by a meter or more every year. Rapid evaporation is due to the extreme heat and the ultra-salinity of the water. The salt content is as much as ten times that of an ocean.

Though many in the science world refuse to believe this, the area hasn't always been so barren, putrid, smelly, or dead. At one time, according to the Bible, this region was lush, habitable, and desirable—at least from Lot's view (Genesis 13:10).

When I think of this area, I do so biblically, historically, medicinally, and prophetically. Let me explain.

Biblically

Many stories in the Bible took place in this region: David hid from Saul (1 Samuel 23:29), Elijah ascended to heaven in a chariot of fire (2 Kings 2:4), the war of the kings (Genesis 14:3), Israel crossed the Jordan (Joshua 3:14–16), and Jesus was baptized (John 1:23, 29–34) by John just about where the Jordan enters the Dead Sea. Also, many of Jesus's works and miracles happened in neighboring Jericho, "the oldest city in the world."

Historically

Jewish and Israeli history record two events of great importance. One happened at Masada. This mount is the southern palace site of Herod the Great and borders the Dead Sea. The second item is recent, and it has been called the most significant find of the twentieth century. We're talking about the discovery of the Dead Sea Scrolls in the Qumran caves, located near the northern bank of the Dead Sea. Found in 1947, these scrolls are copies of biblical manuscripts that further authenticate the Bible's trustworthiness. They are kept in the Shrine of the Book Monument in the Israeli Museum.

Medicinally

Because of the mineral content in the sea and in the area around it, many people descend on this region for its healing qualities. A float in the sea or covering your body in the black mud are thought to be helpful. You've probably seen aspiring entrepreneurs in your local mall selling beauty products from the Dead Sea.

When you go to the Holy Land, you have to float in this sea, at least once. The water's beauty and your body's buoyancy are both quite amazing.

Prophetically

The Salt Sea is mentioned in the prophetic writings of Ezekiel and Zechariah. Ezekiel recalls how he foresaw a time when the sea would be transformed from death to life, from ultra-salty waters that cannot sustain life to fresh waters filled with all types of creatures and vegetation (Ezekiel 47:1–10, Zechariah 14:8).

Again, according to the biblical record, this region was once vibrant, lush, and full of life. It was well watered everywhere. It was only after God rained down His judgment on Sodom and Gomorrah that the area became a wasteland and the sea became a hyper-saline lake. However, during the Millennial Reign of the Messiah after the great tribulation and Christ's Second Coming, this area will return to her original status.

Here, we are focusing on Sodom and the story recorded in Genesis 13, 14, and 19. Lot is the nephew of Abraham, and after their two clans couldn't get along, they are forced to separate. Wise and mature Abraham, the much more spiritual of the two, lets Lot choose where he wants to settle. Lot chose "the well-watered plains of Jordan" (Genesis 13:10), and honestly, things went downhill from there. God finally had enough and was about to judge this land and her people. Before judgment fell, an angel appeared to Lot and told him to gather up his family and get out, and don't turn around. Lot's wife thought she could disregard the angel's warning, and when she turned around to survey the city's destruction, God judged her immediately by turning her into a pillar of salt.

Mount Sodom is a salt rock mound located in the southeast corner of the Dead Sea. Its slopes are covered with tall formations of salt that look like pillars or statues. These formations are called by many locals and guides "Lot's Wife," in reference to the Biblical story.

Noting that, surely there are some "sayings from Sodom" or some "lessons from Lot" we would do well to learn. Let me recount three ideas.

Lot's Choice of Sodom was Wrong on Many Fronts

When he chose where to plant his family, raise his children, and earn his living, Lot failed miserably. Sure, Sodom was a great place to raise cattle, but not children. Sodom was a grand place for money, just not for morals. Lot made a decision that was pleasing to the eye but not the heart.

When Lot *saw* this land, he *desired* it and *chose* it. That has always been part of the enemy's strategy. It worked on Eve, Samson, David, and Lot. It's worked on many of us too. If you read the surrounding texts about Lot and Abraham, Uncle Abe was always building altars. Lot never did. Learn this lesson: When your devotions are weak and your desires are worldly, your decisions will be wrong.

After Lot Chose Sodom, His Life Got Progressively Worse

Did you note the change of status mentioned in Genesis about Lot and Sodom? In 13:12, he "moved his tents as far as Sodom." In 14:12, Lot was "living in Sodom," and by the time you get to 19:1, he is "sitting in the gate of Sodom." That is so clear in how the enemy works and how sin affects us. He was a "friend of the world" (James 4:4), he "loved the world" (1 John 2:15), and he was "conformed to the world" (Romans 12:1–2). All the devil wants us to do is veer, then we become vulnerable, and finally we're a victim.

The words of the psalmist are key here: "How blessed is the man who does not walk in the counsel of the wicked, nor stand in the path of sinners, nor sit in the seat of the scoffers!" (Psalm 1:1). This is not a progression; it's a regression.

As you read these words, it may remind you of a choice or decision you made long ago or in your not-so-distant past. Know this: God's goodness can bring you to repentance; you don't have to stay marred up in bad decisions. (Note, when making crucial decisions for your family and your future, never make them based on money alone. What are the marriage implications, moral implications, and ministry implications?)

Lot's Life Is Marked by Loss

Friends, it never pays to get out of God's will; Lot's life is like a flashing sign, reminding all of this tragedy. Lot lost his testimony. Here was this "righteous" man (2 Peter 2:7–8), living in the midst of moral decay, and he couldn't influence a handful of people for his God. If just ten saved folks could have been found in Sodom, it would have stopped the fires of judgment, but they weren't to be found. Why? Lot's testimony was so messed up, he lost his influence for the Lord. Ouch.

Lot lost his family. His two sons-in-law died in judgment, his wife so loved her life she "looked back" and became a "pillar of salt" (19:26), and his daughters were so messed up from living in Sodom, they got their father drunk and slept with him so they could have children (19:30–38).

Lot lost his possessions. When judgment comes, it affects everyone and everything; Lot lost it all. He started out this journey as a pilgrim, but he ended as a pagan. While with Abraham, he was "looking for a city," he ended up in a cave. It's so sad when people have a saved soul but a lost life.

Don't let that describe you. Remember Lot, his life, and his wife.

Exploration Guide

N
W — E
S

1. Where is the Dead Sea located, and what are some of its unique features?
2. How was this region described prior to God's judgment?
3. Who was Lot? What do you know of his life, family, offspring, worship, and so on?
4. It's been said, "We make our decisions, then they make us." How did this play out in Lot's life?
5. Things for Lot got progressively worse. Do you recall a time in your life or family when a similar thing happened?

Mount Moriah

Genesis 22

I love the city of Jerusalem, and you should as well. 1 Kings 11:13 declares that God has "chosen" Jerusalem for His purposes, and Psalm 87 says He loves that place above all others. That's quite a statement and endorsement.

Many ancient maps will place Jerusalem in the center of the world, and I think they are right to do so. God loves to talk about this amazing place. In fact, we read about Jerusalem 814 times in the Bible.

Most of the tours of this city begin on the Mount of Olives. From this vantage point, you can see the Old City of Jerusalem, Temple Mount, Eastern Gate, Gethsemane, City of David, and the iconic image of the Dome of the Rock. As you stand on one mountain, you can actually see two others: Moriah and Scopus.

As one looks toward the Temple Mount from the Mount of Olives, two structures stand out. To the left is the Al Aqsa Mosque, and to the right is the Dome of the Rock. This beautiful structure is an Islamic shrine that was the first Muslim architectural masterpiece, built in AD 687, about fifty years after the death of Muhammad.

Beneath this impressive golden dome is a rock (hence, the Dome of the Rock). Muslims believe this is where Muhammad ascended, and Jews and Christians believe this is where God told Abraham to offer Isaac as a burnt offering. This sacrificial offering was to take place on Mount Moriah.

It's interesting to me that the mount called Moriah is mentioned only twice in scripture. It is the place of sacrifice where God told

Abraham to take and offer his son (Genesis 22:2), and it is the location where the Lord told Solomon to build the temple (2 Chronicles 3:1). However, it is worth noting that Golgotha is also part of this mountain range. In fact, just outside the modern city walls is an area called Gordon's Calvary. In this area are a skull hill, a garden, a wine press, and a tomb. If this is the location of Jesus's death, then it is less than twenty-five hundred feet from where Abraham took Isaac and where Solomon built his Temple: all on Mount Moriah.

Genesis 22 is one of those high-water marks of scripture. Not that any of them are bad, but some are more memorable than others. I think you'll agree.

The story of Abraham and Isaac has many themes and strikes many chords. In it, God tested Abraham. I'm convinced of this: A life that hasn't been tested can't be trusted. We've really not been tested until we are asked to bear the unbearable, do the unreasonable, and believe the impossible. True faith lives by revelation, not explanation.

This story is also about worship. Genesis 22 is not your average worship service. When we think of worship, we often imagine bulletins, candles, songs, ordinances, and a formal gathering; none of those things are present here, but it's called worship. The word Moses used when writing this account is interesting. It's the same word used when Lot bows before two angels (Genesis 19:1), Joseph saw sheaves "fall" before his sheaf (Genesis 37), Ruth would "bow" before Boaz (Ruth 2), and David "falls down" before Saul (1 Samuel 24).

I might be a little biased, but as a pastor, I'm convinced we oftentimes get it wrong when it comes to worship. Genuine worship requires sacrifice, obedience, preparation, faith, and an understanding of Who God is, what He said, and what He can do; none of that is about hymns, choruses, lights, or comfortable seating. Our worship services would change radically if this were our template.

Finally, the story is about faith. Abraham responds in obedience to God's call. There are no ifs, and, or buts; just a belief in God's perfect plan. The word *Moriah* means "foreseen by Jehovah," and even though Abraham couldn't see all that this command meant, he knew God could. Abraham had faith that he would have a child, even in his old age, and now, he had faith that even if Isaac were slain, God could raise him up again (Romans 4:19–21, Hebrews 11:17–19).

Genesis 22 has been likened to a movie trailer about a coming attraction, one that would happen two thousand years later on the same mountain. One pastor called this a dress rehearsal for Calvary. The movie is good, really good, but the book is better.

Where Is Moriah Located?

Back away from Moriah for a moment. "God created the heavens and the earth" (Genesis 1:1). Think for a moment of our universe:

- There are 100 million galaxies (that we know of).
- One of these is our galaxy, the Milky Way.
- Our galaxy is a hundred thousand light years across, from rim to rim.
- In this galaxy, our little sun is 93 million miles away.
- Orbiting around this sun, in amazingly accurate precision, are eight planets (there used to be nine).
- Of these planets, one is the earth.
- The earth is the Lord's (Psalm 24).
- On earth, God has chosen one area of land for His purpose.
- In that land, God has a city.
- In that city, there are multiple mountains and valleys.
- Right in the center of the Old City of Jerusalem runs the limestone ridge of Mount Moriah.

The mountain is the focal point of all history: past, present, and future. Isaac was taken there, the Temple was built there, Jesus was crucified there, and Christ will one day reign there. This location is not accidental or incidental; it is providential, foreseen by the Lord. God's world, God's earth, God's land, God's city, God's mountain are all part of God's plan.

13

Why Was Moriah Such a Symbolic Place?

In so many ways, what happens to Isaac is a picture of what happens to Jesus. Learn this about Abraham's son and God's son:

- Their coming was prophesied (Genesis 18; Isaiah 7:14).
- Their births were preset (Genesis 18, 21; Galatians 4:4).
- Their names were divinely given (Genesis 17:19, 21; Matthew 1:21).
- Their conception was a miracle (Genesis 13:14; Luke 1:34; Isaiah 7:14).
- They were greatly loved by Father (Genesis 22:2; Luke 4:22; John 17:23).
- They were the only true Son (Genesis 22:2; John 3:16).
- They were offered as a sacrifice (Genesis 22:2; 2 Corinthians 5:21).
- They were raised from dead (Genesis 22:4; 1 Corinthians 15:3–4).

Of course, Isaac's resurrection was more symbolic, on the third day, but God could raise him (Hebrews 11:19)

In so many ways, Isaac and this story remind us of Jesus and his actual death and resurrection years later. Another interesting note: After Moriah, we don't see Isaac until we meet his bride Rebekah. Jesus left earth after His death, resurrection, and ascension; the next time we will see Him, He will be coming to meet His bride. Can I get an amen?

What are Moriah's Main Lessons?

There are many lessons related to this story, but I want to repeat something said earlier: Mount Moriah is only mentioned twice in scripture by name, but it is alluded to at least one other place. One day, Jesus was ministering and teaching (the Bible says to some "Jews"). Jesus brought up their Patriarch Abraham, and He said, "Your Father Abraham rejoiced to see My day and he saw it and was glad" (John 8:56). When and where did Abraham see Jesus and rejoice? No doubt he did on Mount Moriah. In fact, in Isaac's miraculous birth, he saw Christ's birth; in Isaac's willingness to obey, he saw Christ's obedience; in Isaac's marriage, he saw the day of Christ coming for His bride. Abraham saw this and rejoiced. He saw the substitute caught in the thicket; he rejoiced in this and was glad.

Genesis 22 and the story of Mount Moriah are worth reading over and over. Many years after this event, the writer of Hebrews was admonishing some Jews and used many examples of their ancestors to do it. One of those examples was Abraham and Isaac, and the difficult and dark day at Moriah. That writer reminded his readers, and I want to admonish you: believe God. No, really, believe God

- when you don't know where (Hebrews 11:8),
- when you don't know when (Hebrews 11:9–10, 13–16)
- when you don't know how (Hebrews 11:11–12), and
- when you don't know why (Hebrews 11:17–19), and
- you too will be able to rejoice and be glad.

Exploration Guide

1. Where is Mount Moriah located, and why is it so significant?
2. If you've been to Jerusalem, what was your favorite site to visit? Why?
3. Genesis 22 has been called "a dress rehearsal for Calvary." What does that mean?
4. Discuss a time or season in your life when you were being tested.
5. Abraham approached Moriah as an opportunity to worship. What are some ways we can prepare for worship?
6. Read John 8:48–59. Focus on verse 56. What does this mean?
7. Read Hebrews 11:8–19 about Abraham. How does his obedience challenge you?

Mount Sinai (Horeb)

Exodus 19–20

In each of our chapters, we will learn about our Christian life and what it means to be a growing follower of the Lord. Most of the mountains and hills and valleys we are viewing are in Israel or elsewhere in the Holy Land. A few we will see are not, but they are too important to omit. Surely Mount Sinai fits this description.

Several sites have been suggested as the mountain of God. Where this mountain is and where this event happened is not nearly as important as what transpires there. Really, this is true all over the land.

The Bible uses the term *Sinai* for the region, the mountain, and the entire wilderness area. There are times when Moses, the human author of the five Books of the Law, would use "the Mount," sometimes "the Mountain of God," and at times "the mount of the Lord." On some occasions, the word "Horeb" is used. It appears that the terms are synonyms. For clarity, it seems best to use Horeb as the specific peak where God manifested Himself to Moses.

This area is located in the south-central part of the Sinai Peninsula, between the Gulf of Suez and the Gulf of Aqaba. It would be north of the main body of the Red Sea.

On a few occasions in scripture, this region is called the "Wilderness of Sin," but this has nothing to do with a description of human depravity. (To preach that or read that into this text is not proper hermeneutics. I don't care who preached it. Rant over.)

The book of Exodus is a prophetic picture of coming redemption. God raises up a Savior (Moses), who brings the Hebrew people out of bondage; the only way out was by blood. Then, he shows the people how to walk and how to worship. The truth is, they came out of Egypt in a night, but it would take the rest of their lives to get Egypt out of them.

To aid the people in their growth and sanctification, God gave them His laws. Remember, God's law does not save sinners; it reveals the sinfulness of our heart and our need for a Savior. The law is likened to a mirror that reveals how dirty we are, but it is not a basin that provides our cleansing. Only Jesus can do that.

Don't forget these texts about God's law and its purpose:

- "The law ... can never ... make perfect" (Hebrews 10:1).
- "For the law is our tutor to lead us to Christ" (Galatians 3:24).
- "For through the law comes the knowledge of sin" (Romans 3:20).
- "For we contend that man is justified apart from works of the law" (Romans 3:28).
- "For I do not nullify the grace of God, for if righteousness comes through the law, then Christ died needlessly" (Galatians 2:21).

But God did call for Moses to meet Him on the mount, and He did give him His word(s) to record and to teach to others. Sinai, no doubt, is a specific and a special place. Here is a probing question for all of us: "Do I have a special place where I meet with God and receive His word and instructions for life?"

In that sense, what might we learn from these verses and this location?

❖ Do you have a place where you meet with God (19:3)?

Moses is going up the mount to meet with his Lord. It's a time of personal interaction and worship. You could call it his quiet time, but it sounds pretty noisy.

❖ Do you have a place to remember and recount God's faithfulness (19:4)? Moses had a past with God, and he had seen his Lord work time and again. He recalls the series of plagues, the night of the Exodus, the Passover lamb, and how God's power was manifested at the Red Sea.

Roger D. Mardis

Because he had seen God work before, he knew He would again. Here's a great reminder: don't forget in the dark what God taught you in the light.

❖ Do you have place to respond in obedience (19:5–8)?
My daddy used to say, "I'm not talking just to hear myself speak." I can imagine God often thought the same. God has given us His Word so we can respond in obedience.

❖ Do you have a place of cleansing to be prepared to meet God in worship (19:10–11)?
As I pen these words, it convicts me; do I approach my daily time with the Lord in a serious or a subtle way? Do I remove worldly distractions? Is my television turned off and my phone silenced? Imagine how you would prepare if you were meeting with a dignitary, a noteworthy figure, or a president. People, we are meeting with the Lord.

❖ Do you have a place of reverence and respect for the things of God (19:12–15)?
Earlier God had told Moses to take his shoes off, he was on holy ground. If we approached our time with the Lord with the same respect, we may get better results.

❖ Do you have a place to be in awe of God (19:16)?
In our day, we seem to have lost the idea of what it means to fear the Lord. Here the Israelites "trembled" before God. I often wonder if we even know what it means today to fear the Lord. We are in a sad place.

As you perhaps know, once Moses got the tablets, he came down from the mount, only to find the people disobeying God and worshipping a golden calf (Exodus 32). In his frustration and anger, Moses threw the tablets down and broke them. The laws the Israelites broke with their heart, Moses broke with his hands.

Because the tablets had to be replaced, Moses climbed Sinai yet again, and not only are the commands rewritten, God's mercy is reiterated. When the Lord passed by in front of Moses, He spoke

18

these words: "The Lord, the Lord God, compassionate and gracious, slow to anger, and abounding in lovingkindness and truth; who keeps lovingkindness for thousands, who forgives iniquity, transgressions and sin" (34:6–7a). As a result, Moses fell on his face and worshipped.

When Moses descended from Mount Sinai, the Bible says his face was aglow; it shone (34:29–35). He had met with the Lord, and now Moses was coming back a different man. Now, I am not saying that when we learn to have a dynamic time with Christ, our faces will also shine, but I am saying that there will be a holy glow of God on you, and people will know you have been with Jesus.

In fact, Acts 4:13 says of Peter and John, "Now as they [the religious onlookers] observed the confidence of Peter and John and understood that they were untrained and uneducated men, they were amazed and began to recognize them as having been with Jesus."

So I challenge you to have a Mount Sinai in your daily life; a place where you meet with the Lord, get instruction from His Word, and learn to put it into practice. When you do that, your life will take on a different look.

Exploration Guide

1. Have you ever broken a law? What happened?
2. What is the purpose of God's law?
3. Discuss your daily time with the Lord; how is it formatted? When? Where? What are your goals?
4. Moses's time with the Lord radically changed him. What traits do you wish to develop from spending time with the Lord?
5. Take some time to think over Hebrews 10, Galatians 3, and Romans 3.

Valley of Eshcol

Numbers 13, 32

The Valley of Eshcol is in "Canaan Land," close to Hebron. I reference Canaan because this site is best noted as the location where the twelve Israeli spies visited and found great clusters of fruit (Numbers 13:23–24). The name *Eshcol* actually means "cluster" or "valley of grapes." More than likely, this area derived its name from the young Amorite chief who allied with Abraham in retrieving Lot from the capture of Chedorlaomer and his armies in Dan.

We come to know this valley when Moses permits twelve spies to go into the Land of Canaan and check it out. This was not God's plan or intention. He had already given them the land, but God allows this maneuver to take place to teach them a lesson and reveal the faithlessness of their hearts. What was the land like? How many people were there (for us to fight)? Were they strong or weak? Was the land good or bad? Were their cities fortified or open? Was the land suitable for our crops?

In many ways, these questions are normal and what we would call due diligence. However, when you read the whole story (Deuteronomy 1), you find that the real issue is unbelief and a lack of faith in what God said. Moses went so far as to call it outright rebellion, and the people grumbled (sounds like many Baptists I know).

Before we jump into this story, let me make two statements. First, Canaan is not an illustration of heaven, regardless of what some preachers say, singers sing, and songwriters write. Canaan is a reminder of the opportunity believers have of the Spirit-filled life;

such a life is faithful and fruitful. Second, we all love the names of Joshua (Hoshea) and Caleb. In fact, I know many people who have these names. However, no one names their son after any of the other ten spies, and you probably don't even recall their names. Neither do I, and I'm writing about them. There is something to be said for that, my friends. If you want people to remember you and take note of your name, you better be a person of faith.

Moses had told the spies, "Bring me back some of the fruit in the land." And when they did, the fruit was so large and heavy that two men had to carry it on a pole. They also brought pomegranates and figs. The place where these fruits were cut and gathered was called the Valley of Eshcol.

What followed after this forty-day time of exploration was a report ... and a rebellion. Once back to Kadesh, the twelve spies talked about their trip: what they did, saw, felt, and experienced. (Similar to when someone returns home from a mission trip.) As the spies recounted the story, there are some key phrases that stand out. "Certainly" (v. 27) was a great reply. The land is beautiful and productive, and the harvest is rewarding. This is a land flowing with milk (goats) and honey (from dates, not bees), and it is fruitful.

Nevertheless, that was not the faith response that Moses wanted. "There are giant cities, giant walls, and giant people, and we are nothing compared to them." Instead of seeing the opportunity, they saw opposition, and instead of living in faith, they were dominated by fear. Disbelief and fear will halt one's progress in any venture quicker than anything. Many a church is located on the corner of Fear Avenue and Disbelief Way. If we can name churches after Corinth, why isn't there a Grasshopper Community Fellowship (just sayin')?

The problem with the committee's report is spelled out in two ideas: Caleb: "We should by all means," and the crowd: "We are not able," and the result is a "bad report" (v. 32), and the congregation of people "cried, wept ... and grumbled" (14:1–2). Instead of trusting in what God had said and promised, they preferred to hike back to Egypt (14:4). Come to think of it, I believe I pastored a group (or two) like this.

21

Noting this backdrop, Eshcol says many things to us.

It Is Noted as a Place of Fruit (Numbers 13:23–24)

Canaan was indeed a fruitful and productive land that was flowing with milk and honey. Eshcol is a location in the Promised Land, but it reminds us that as followers of Christ, we are to have a productive life and be fruitful.

In John 15, Jesus picks up on this theme and speaks of Himself being the true Vine and His Father is the Vine Dresser. He then goes into a lesson in pomology (the study of fruit). There are several key truths He shares. There are levels of fruit growing. Jesus says, "fruit ... more fruit ... much fruit" (John 15:2, 5). Which of these bests describes your life? Or mine? Our churches? Every believer is to live a fruitful, Spirit-filled life.

There are times we need pruning. If my life is not bearing proper fruit in abundance, then there is a problem, and Jesus wants to help me fix the problem. So he may "take away, prune or clean." Every winter at my home in Alabama, I have a job to do in cutting back my rose bushes and crepe myrtles. It's tiring, laborious, and time consuming. At times, it gets messy and sticky. However, it's worthwhile when my beautiful bushes come alive in spring. Our gracious Lord does the same for us.

The real key is abiding. No less than ten times in this passage, Jesus speaks of our abiding in Him. When we abide in the Lord, we will bear fruit (v. 4), grow in our faith (v. 5), and have a successful prayer life (v. 10). Truly, "apart from Him we can do nothing" (v. 5b). When I am living in communion and close fellowship with my Lord, the "fruit" mentioned in Galatians 5:22–23 will be seen in my life.

It Is Recounted as a Place of Failure (Numbers 32:1–15)

You would think that the grave sins of these people would be such a lesson and warning that everyone would learn from them. However, fortysomething years later, we are still singing this song: the second verse. As a new generation of people moved forward in faith into

Canaan Land, two and a half of the tribes decided to stay on the other side of the Jordan. They came as far as the river but then stopped. Some people choose to live on the outskirts of God's blessing and within sight of His will. I once heard it said that partial obedience is disobedience. Listen to how this reads:

Now why are you discouraging the sons of Israel from crossing over into the land which the Lord has given them? This is what your fathers did when I sent them from Kadesh-barnea to see the land. For when they went up to the valley of Eshcol and saw the land, they discouraged the sons of Israel so that they did not go into the land which the Lord had given them. So the Lord's anger burned in that day, and He swore, saying, "None of the men who came up from Egypt, from twenty years old and upward, shall see the land which I swore to Abraham, to Isaac and to Jacob; for they did not follow Me fully, except Caleb the son of Jephunneh the Kenizzite and Joshua the son of Nun, for they have followed the Lord fully." So the Lord's anger burned against Israel, and He made them wander in the wilderness forty years, until the entire generation of those who had done evil in the sight of the Lord was destroyed. (Numbers 32:7–13)

Like fathers, like sons. Now the new generation of people are walking in the same steps of disobedience, and Moses calls them out.

Now behold, you have risen up in your fathers' place, a brood of sinful men, to add still more to the burning anger of the Lord against Israel. For if you turn away from following Him, He will once more abandon them in the wilderness, and you will destroy all these people. (Numbers 32:14–15)

What for these people should have been a great reminder of fruitfulness, became a time of failure, just like their ancestors.

It Is a Place of Faith (Numbers 13:30–31)

Our lives are going to look like either Caleb's or the crowd's. It will either be one of faith or one of failure. I can either claim God's promises and live an obedient, Spirit-filled life that is faith filled and fruit bearing, or I can disobey the Lord's Word and wander in unbelief and failure. I have to tell you, I'm not interested in going back to Egypt, wandering in the wilderness, camping out on the border of Canaan, or living an unproductive life. I want to abide in my Lord and abound in His favor. How about you?

Caleb and his co-laborer Joshua were not in the majority, but they were right. When the report came back about the new land and its challenges, they were on the wrong side of the committee but the right side of the Lord. There are times when we are in the minority, maybe even alone, but they obeyed the Lord and His Word and, in the end, God vindicated them, and He will do the same for you.

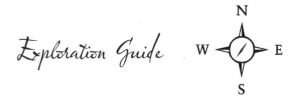

Exploration Guide

1. When you hear the word "Canaan," what ideas or images come to mind?
2. In what ways is Numbers 13 a story of unbelief?
3. Can you recall a situation when the majority made a major blunder? Discuss.
4. What are the fruits you hope people see evidenced in your life? Do they?
5. History has a way of repeating itself. How did that happen in this story? Has that ever happened to you?
6. What does it mean to "abide" in Christ? Find passages where this verse is used.

Mount Nebo

Deuteronomy 32, 34

I have personally visited the location of most of the hills and valleys listed in this book, with the exception of a few. Though I've seen Mount Nebo many times, I've not actually been there. We learn about this mount from the writings and life of Moses. Maybe I should say from his writings and his death.

Mount Nebo is located on the Jordan side of the Dead Sea, across from Jericho. Mount Nebo is the site where God allowed Moses to *view* the Promised Land, but he wasn't allowed to *enter*. The Lawgiver and the leader couldn't enter the land; surely that makes you ask, why not?

Moses is one of the leading characters of the Old Testament, and he is referenced many times in the New Testament. The entirety of his life was quite amazing. Think of this: As a newborn, he was saved by his mother and sister from Pharaoh's order to kill all the Israelite babies. He was raised and schooled in the finest ways of the Egyptians and was trained by God on the backside of the desert. He performed many miracles by God's power prior to the Exodus and led a million people out of slavery and into freedom. He saw the Red Sea part, got water out of a rock, received the Law of God, and knew God face to face (Deuteronomy 34:10). Moses had a pretty impressive resumé.

He also had some shortcomings. He murdered a guy. He was unwise at times in his work. He had episodes of anger and fits of frustration. His faith at times faltered. He complained to God about his task, and oh, yeah, he got so prideful one day that he rebelled against God's commands, and it cost him his life. Really? Really.

Let me remind you of what happened. God had used Moses to get water from a rock in the earlier days of their pilgrimage (Exodus 17), and now the crowd was complaining again because of thirst. God tells Moses to "speak" to the rock, but Moses disobeys and instead strikes the rock like before. Seems as if Moses and Aaron wanted a little glory for themselves, and it cost them dearly.

Friend, God will not share His glory with any other, including Moses (nor me, nor you, nor anyone). Listen to God's response: "Because you have not believed Me, to treat Me as Holy in the sight of the sons of Israel, therefore you shall not bring this assembly into the Land which I have given them" (Numbers 20:12). Moses committed a sin that led to his death.

There are many lessons we should draw from this story and from this serious lack of restraint on Moses's part. What might we learn?

God Takes Rebellion Seriously

He always has, and He always will. In fact, there seems to be a more serious reaction when it involves those in positions of authority or leadership. Moses didn't just get prideful and take matters into his own hands; he disobeyed God's clear instruction. He rebelled. And did you know this? God says that "rebellion is as the sin of witchcraft" (1 Samuel 15:23). When we rebel against God's clear commands, it's as if we are speaking a curse onto our life. That proved serious to Moses, and it is to us as well.

To Strike the Rock a Second Time Spoiled the Type

Years later, the apostle Paul reconnected this story; he writes, "And they all drank the same spiritual drink, for they were drinking from a spiritual rock which followed them, and the rock was Christ" (1 Corinthians 10:4). Jesus Christ was and is our true Rock. The first time Moses struck the rock, it pointed to Calvary, but Jesus wouldn't need to be "struck" (crucified) again. All one has to do now is "speak to the rock"; you might call that prayer. Christ died once and for all, and now all we need to do is call upon Him. God had to react severely because Moses violated the type. (A biblical type is something stated or pictured but it represents so much more. It is given in the Old Testament and finds its fulfillment in the New Testament).

Moses, the Lawgiver, Was Not Enough

In striking the rock and destroying the type, Moses was not only revealing Who God was, he was revealing his own limitations. The law will never justify us by itself. The law might reveal sin, but it certainly will not remove it; only Jesus can do that.

The writer of Hebrews highlights this very well. Chapter 10 reminds us, "The Law can never make perfect" (v. 1), "it is impossible for the blood of bulls and goats to take away sin" (v. 4), "sacrifices ... can never take away sins" (v. 11). But look at v. 14: "For by one offering He [Jesus] has perfected for all time those who are sanctified." So waver not, my friend, "for He who promised is faithful" (v. 23).

God knew it would take a Joshua ("Yahweh Is Salvation") to lead the people to their earthly rest, as only Jesus leads us to spiritual rest. "For what the law could never do ... God did, sending His own Son" (Romans 8:3).

Moses Committed a Sin unto Death

Moses was 120 years of age when he died, but scripture says of him, "his eyes were not dim nor his vigor abated" (Deuteronomy 34:7). What does that mean? Moses was older, but he was certainly not old, by the standards of his day. He could still see, hear, and get around. In fact, he was strong enough to still climb mountains: "He went up to Mt. Nebo to the top of Pisgah" (Deuteronomy 34:1).

In all actuality, Moses committed what John would years later call "a sin that leads to death" (1 John 5:16). This is what killed Ananias and Sapphira in Acts 5, Herod in Acts 12, and some believers from Corinth in 1 Corinthians 11. Again, I remind you, rebelling against God and robbing Him of His rightful glory is a serious offense.

Only God Attended Moses's Funeral

Have you noticed how society has a way of elevating people or personalities beyond their due? We do that for athletes and actors, musicians and ministers, businesspeople and Bible scholars. Need I remind you that we are all human, we all have flaws, no one is perfect, each of us is finite or temporary.

Surely God knew that and knows that. I'm convinced that's why only He was there when Moses died. See, as much as people fussed and complained to Moses while he lived, once he was gone, it was different.

No doubt the people would have carried Moses's body around, idolized it, and worshiped it. (If you don't believe people do that, visit the Holy Land; idolatry there is real, and it is heartbreaking.) We do read in Jude 9 that Michael the Archangel "argued with Satan about the body of Moses." Hmmm.

Moses Did Ultimately Visit the Promised Land

In Deuteronomy, Moses prayed and asked God to "change His mind" and let him enter the Promised Land. God refused (Deuteronomy 3:21–29). Later, however, Moses and Elijah join Jesus and His inner circle on another mountain, the Mount of Transfiguration. Think of it like this: the Law (Moses) and the Prophets (Elijah) got to the Land of Promise by Grace (Jesus). Moses left this world after a natural death and burial. Elijah was transported alive to glory. One of those two ways is how we will all leave.

Moses Surely Chuckled in His Grave over the People's Response to His Death

Practically from day one, this massive gathering of people was fussing, complaining, and finger-pointing (toward him, I assume).

Go back and read the books of Exodus, Numbers, and Deuteronomy; with pen or highlighter in hand, mark the times the people "murmured."

Grammarians call that kind of word onomatopoeia. It is the formation of words by sounds. You pronounce it like it sounds. That's what murmuring and complaining is: a lot of unnecessary noise. I hope you are never guilty of that at work, in church or on social media.

But look at these people now. Their murmuring has become mourning. They wept and cried for Moses for thirty days. What a difference a funeral made.

It does behoove me to say, I hope we all live in such a way that when we're gone, people miss us and aren't rejoicing.

Everybody Is Replaceable, Even Moses

Notice how the Pentateuch (the five books of Moses) ends. The record says that there was no prophet like Moses; he spoke to God face to face; he performed many signs and wonders; he displayed mighty power (Deuteronomy 34:10–12). But Moses was now gone, and Joshua was their new leader. Every great leader will one day need to be replaced, and life will go on.

You've probably heard the story of the young executive who was too big for his britches and thought he could never be replaced. His boss, made aware of such an idea, called him into his office, where he had a bucket of water on his desk. He was about to teach the young man a valuable lesson. "You want to know how much you'll be missed," he asked, "or how long it will take us to replace you? Stick your fist into this bucket of water." The younger man did so. "Now pull it out. Did you see how quickly that place where your fist was filled in? That's how quick you will be replaced if this inflated attitude continues. Now, get back to work."

Humbling, right?

People, circumstances, and time have a way of humbling and replacing us all.

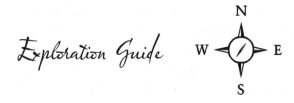

Exploration Guide

1. What stories in Moses's life stand out most to you? Why?
2. Why was "striking the rock" such a serious sin?
3. Have you ever known someone who committed the sin unto death?
4. Why do you think God buried Moses as He did?
5. Is there any significance in Moses and Elijah meeting Jesus years later in the Promised Land?

Valley of Achor (Trouble)

Joshua 7

The book of Joshua is a favorite to many preachers, including me. Chapters 6 and 7 graphically illustrate the theme of this book. There are hills and valleys, highs and lows, wins and losses. Think of this: Jericho is conquered in a most unconventional way. Surely Ai will be next. Instead, the great win is followed by a humiliating defeat. High points are often tempered by low ones.

I saw this firsthand on many occasions as a pastor. One such time is still fresh in my mind. I had led a young, energetic, and fruitful couple to Christ. However, after their fourth child was born, the mother had a massive stroke and later died. It was a crushing and confusing time for family, community, and church. Think of that. Right after one of life's greatest highs was a massive low. I've had many moments like that, and I'm sure you have as well.

So did Joshua. So did Israel. So did Achan. Think of the early events of the book of Joshua. Moses has died, and young Joshua is now in charge. The Promised Land is checked out, but only two spies brought back a good report. (By the way, many people name their sons after Joshua and Caleb, but can you name one of the other ten?) Israel crosses the Jordan after God's miraculous work. Jericho is conquered. Rahab is rescued along with her family. Win, win, win, until you get to chapter 7 and the city of Ai.

Interestingly, *Ai* means "ruin" or "heap." It was almost the ruin of Joshua's newly appointed leadership. It was a place of ruin for Achan and his family. It suffered complete ruin; all of her inhabitants were killed. The city was burned, and it was left a heap of destruction. They hung the king. Listen to God's Word:

Now when Israel had finished killing all the inhabitants of Ai in the field in the wilderness where they pursued them, and all of them were fallen by the edge of the sword until they were destroyed, then all Israel returned to Ai and struck it with the edge of the sword. All who fell that day, both men and women, were 12,000—all the people of Ai. For Joshua did not withdraw his hand with which he stretched out the javelin until he had utterly destroyed all the inhabitants of Ai. Israel took only the cattle and the spoil of that city as plunder for themselves, according to the word of the LORD which He had commanded Joshua. So Joshua burned Ai and made it a heap forever, a desolation until this day. He hanged the king of Ai on a tree until evening; and at sunset Joshua gave command and they took his body down from the tree and threw it at the entrance of the city gate, and raised over it a great heap of stones *that stands* to this day. (Joshua 7:24–29)

Right after this, what does Joshua do? He builds an altar to the Lord on Mount Ebal. Amazing. Win, loss. Valley, mountain. Dear reader, God wants us to learn something here. Don't stay in Achor; hurry and get to Ebal.

Let's focus for a moment on the Valley of Achor (7:26). The word *achor* means trouble, affliction, or taboo. Here, Achan and his family were stoned to death. Achor became the subject of prophetic utterances in Isaiah 65:10 and in Hosea 2:15. Hosea used a unique play on words when he said God can turn your trouble (Achor) into a door of hope.

How does one find such hope in a world that appears increasingly hopeless?

That question reminds me of this story: There was a massive Portuguese ship, ironically named *Save*. On board were fifty-three crewmen, three hundred Portuguese troops, and two hundred Mozambique Africans. The ship ran aground on a sandbar off the coast of East Africa during a storm. While rescue efforts were being made from the shore, a fire broke out on the ship. The fire soon spread to the stored ammunition, and the whole ship exploded into flames. Many of the passengers jumped overboard, only to be attacked by sharks. Those who did make it to shore were threatened by lions roaring in the nearby jungle. At every turn was trouble and hopelessness. No hope on the boat, in the water, or at the shore (and you think you've had a bad week).

If you've not had an Achor moment, hold on. These times come to all of us. The real question is not, have you had one, but rather, what did you learn while there? Let me suggest some great truths to learn.

Transgression

If you aren't familiar with this story, you may want to read Joshua 7. With the conquest of Jericho in the rear-view mirror, surely the small city of Ai would be an easy task. However, their presumptuousness and Achan's disobedience were a lethal combination. This chapter offers us several reminders:

- It is important that we obey the Lord fully (7:1).
- Sinful hearts can become arrogant; we trust ourselves instead of God (7:3).
- When we resort to our own strength or tactics, the results can be devastating and discouraging (7:4–5).
- There are times when we need to quit praying and acting spiritual and start getting right with God (7:6–12).
- We cannot fully enjoy the blessings of God when there is unconfessed sin or unresolved conflict or issues in our life (7:12).
- Ultimately, all of our sin is against the Lord (7:19–20).
- You can be forgiven of your sin and still face the consequences of poor decisions. Ouch (7:24–26).

Chapter 7 is a picture of our transgressions and futile attempts to hide them from God while we lean on our own understanding.

Trouble

As said earlier, Achor means trouble, affliction, or taboo. Trouble is the natural result of transgression. Put another way, it should not surprise us when we encounter seasons of trouble while doing things contrary to God's laws and principles. How many times have you heard, "Are you asking for trouble?"

You marry outside of God's will: trouble.
You buy more house than you can afford: trouble.
You hang out with the wrong crowd: trouble.
You linger too long on the internet: trouble.
You take more painkillers than the doctor prescribed: trouble.
You rebel against the authority of your parents, pastor, or employer: trouble.

I can't begin to tell you the number of times through the years that I did something stupid and had to pay the penalty (the "stupid tax"). Have you?

Again, the key is, what did you learn? See, God **will** put more on you than you can handle, until you learn to trust Him. You better go back and read that again because your favorite TV preacher will not tell you that. In fact, listen to what Paul writes:

For we do not want you to be unaware, brethren, of our affliction which came *to us* in Asia, that we were burdened excessively, beyond our strength, so that we despaired even of life; indeed, we had the sentence of death within ourselves so that we would not trust in ourselves, but in God who raises the dead; who delivered us from so great a *peril of* death, and will deliver *us*, He on whom we have set our hope. And He will yet deliver us. (2 Corinthians 1:8–10)

Paul said, "It was so bad, I thought I was going to die." God had put more on him than he could bear. Why? So he would learn to trust God and not himself. In fact, he said God came through in the past and in the present, and He will in the future. Friend, He will do the same for you. Learn what you must in your current situation, and then put your Achor behind you.

Triumph

Here is the reality: Only God can take our helpless and hopeless situations and bring good from them. In fact, the prophet Hosea would later write, "God will soon restore the fortune and blessing of Israel and her inhabitants—the Valley of Achor [trouble] will soon become a door of hope" (Hosea 2:15). Did you get that? Only with God can your obstacles become an opportunity, your difficulty a door, your trouble a triumph, and your hopelessness … hope.

Hope is that indispensable quality of life. It's been said that we can live forty days without food, three days without water, four minutes without air, but only a few seconds without hope.

Today, let God turn your Achor into a door of hope.

Exploration Guide   W ⟵⊙⟶ E
                              N
                              S

1. How do you define trouble?
2. Recall times when you "got in trouble" and when you were "going through some trouble." Is there a difference?
3. Achan was guilty of disobeying the Lord and in trying to cover up his sin. Have you ever done this? How did it make you feel? Was resolution ever made?
4. Using a Bible dictionary, look up the words *sin*, *iniquity*, and *transgression*. What is the difference in each word?
5. Read 2 Corinthians 1:8–10. What was Paul's "trouble"? How did he feel? How did he respond?
6. Since we know God is sovereign and wise, and He cares for us; what is the purpose for my going through a time of trouble?

Valley of Mizpeh

Joshua 11

Joshua had been born into slavery in Egypt but had been brought out of the house of bondage. He lived through many years of ups and downs and in wandering in the wilderness. He had leaned on Moses so much; he listened to him, and he learned from him, but now Moses was gone.

Joshua so respected Moses; he never expected to replace him.

Remember, Joshua and Caleb, along with ten others, had spied out this new land; it truly was a land of promise, flowing with milk and abundant in honey, but it wasn't just a land to be occupied. It had to be overcome. Battles, enemies, difficulties, and more were there and would have to be faced. In Moses, we had the prospects of the Holy Land, but in Joshua, the possession of it. Moses illustrates the ability of faith, but Joshua the accomplishments.

The book of Joshua in the Old Testament is similar to the book of Acts in the New. Both of these are books of transition. Whereas Acts is between the Gospel declaration and the church age, Joshua is the link between Egypt and the wilderness and the Promised Land. While making this transition, a series of battles would have to be fought and won. So God reminds Joshua to be "strong and courageous" and grow in his "faith"; he will need to if he is to conquer and win.

When you finally read Joshua 6, you begin to see a series of battles. These battles remind me of the threefold enemy I face every day: Jericho (chapter 6) reminds me of the *world*, Ai (chapter 7–8) of the *flesh*, and the coalition of kings and kingdoms of chapters 9–11 of the *devil*. But God gives us the victory over all three. And He will go so far as to make the sun stand still to accomplish His plan (10:12–14).

Notice the enemies: Gibeonites, a Southern alliance, and now a Northern one. This unusual collaboration of many opposing kingdoms not only got Joshua's attention, but it brought some fear to his heart. God's words in 11:6, "stop being afraid," remind me of what He said to Paul (Acts 23:11). Fear is such a clever tool. It not only makes us immovable; it renders us ineffective. And yet, the arsenal of our enemy has a spear of fear, a dart of doubt, and many arrows of adversity.

To combat this attack, God speaks to His man, saying, "Here is what you are to do, and here is what I will do." So in Mizpeh, Israel conquers the enemy until no survivor is left; Joshua did as God had told him (v. 9).

Joshua 10–12 is really an interlude, but it describes what Joshua did and what God did. It's a summary of God's activity and Joshua's obedience. There are times in all of our lives where we need to push pause and be reminded of God's work and our own responses.

In Joshua 11:1–10, General Joshua is at the helm, leading Israel in many battles and facing multiple enemies. These Canaanites and remnants of the Amorites, Hittites, Perizzites, Jebusites, Hivites, and mosquito bites (eh ... just wanted to make sure you were paying attention) sent a massive coalition to confront Joshua. Reading about all these "-ites" reminds me of Pastor R. G. Lee once saying, "all these isms that should be was-ims." Joshua felt the same about all these "ites," and he is about to take them all on.

This also reminds me of the spiritual battles and warfare we all face. The Christian life is not a *playground*; it's a *battleground*, and the souls of people are at stake. What might we learn and apply from this meeting in Mizpeh?

We Must Live by Faith and Not Be Overcome by Fear (11:6)

From the beginning, God had told young Joshua to be "strong and courageous" (1:6–7, 9). Over and over, God reminds Joshua, and the Lord leads them in victory. God had given him the promise of this land (1:4), Joshua had witnessed God's activity with Rahab (2:1–18), God parted the waters of the Jordan for Israel to cross (3:1–4:7), God enabled Israel to defeat Jericho (6:1–21), God got their attention after a defeat at Ai (Ch. 7), God led them to utterly defeat the men of Ai so that "not a man was left in Ai or Bethel" (8:17).

Now, Joshua and Israel are going to have to believe God afresh; He has worked before, and He will work again. In the battles we face, we need to recall the same; the same God Who has worked before will give you strength for today and bright hope for tomorrow.

We Must Remember That It's the Lord's Battle and Not Ours (11:6, 8)

Here is some great news when it comes to the warfare of a believer: This is not just your enemy; it's God's. It's His power, it's His armor, and it will be His victory. In many ways, we are just like Jehoshaphat. Listen to what he said and how God responded: "For we are powerless before this great multitude who are coming up against us; nor do we know what to do, but our eyes are on you." And listen to the response: "King Jehoshaphat, thus says the Lord to you, do not fear or be dismayed because of this multitude, for the battle is not yours but God's" (2 Chronicles 20:12, 15). It would be prideful and foolish to think we could win a spiritual battle on our own.

We Must Totally Renounce the Flesh and Remove the Enemy (11:8b)

God instructed Joshua in what he was to do after the victory. What a command it is: "hamstring their horses and burn their chariots" (11:6). After God wipes out the enemy, look at what Joshua does: "So Joshua did to them as the Lord had told him; he hamstrung their horses and he burned their chariots with fire."

One would think that a dead army would be enough, but just in case, he eliminated their weapons of war. By removing their horses and chariots, their fight-and-flight ability was gone; lingering soldiers and weapons always have a way of resurfacing in a bad (if not worse) manner.

We Must Be Completely Obedient (11:6, 9)

Joshua had learned, and he was still learning. He had to do all God had told him: remove all the enemies, kill all the horses, burn all the chariots. Listen to how it reads: "Joshua captured all the cities of these kings and all their kings, and he struck them with the edge of the sword, and *utterly destroyed them*; just as Moses the servant of the Lord had commanded" (Joshua 11:12, emphasis added). Here is a great truth to remember: "Partial obedience is disobedience." I'm not sure who first said that, but I have come to understand that it is true.

As you begin to gather your possessions and conquer all the land God has provided for you, never forget this: If you're to conquer for Him, you must be consumed with Him, controlled by Him, and clothed with Him; that's what Ephesians 5–6 begins to unfold.

Never forget, there will be little or no success in our spiritual battles unless we make much of His promises and still more of the Promiser Himself. The foes we face are far too great for us—so we look to the One Whose soldiers we are. If we do, no matter how great our weaknesses may be or how formidable our foes are, our Lord will not fail us. Amen.

Exploration Guide   W —◁ ⬥ ▷— E
N
S

1. In what ways is the book of Joshua a book of "transition"?
2. Dig back through Joshua's book and find the many times God tells him to "be strong and courageous." What battles are you currently facing that need your attention and this reminder?
3. Are there times you deal with the emotion of fear? When are those times, and how do you handle them?
4. How have you learned to fight your spiritual battles? Has this been successful?
5. Think of a time in your past where you saw God move, work, or deliver. Why not allow Him to work again as He did before?
6. Think of this line: "There will be little or no success in our spiritual battles unless we make much of His promises and still more of the Promiser Himself." What are some biblical promises you are currently claiming or relying on? What are you expecting your Promiser to do?

Valley of Sorek

Judges 16

Every journey to the Holy Land is unique and special. I've now made many and can tell you that is true. Each time Friends of Nazareth (FON) takes a mission team there, we try to add some new places. One place I have never been to is a place called Sorek. Honestly, I'm not even sure if this area is still inhabited.

Sorek is a place name that means "red grape" (evidently, it was known for its fruitful harvest); it is mentioned in the Bible as a valley where Delilah, Samson's mistress, lived (Judges 16:4). This valley was located on the western side of Jerusalem toward the Great Sea. It is close to Beth Shemesh and the Elah Valley.

Though we know very little of this biblical valley, we do know that Samson went there, and it cost him greatly. We've all known modern people who have boarded the "Sorek Shuttle," only to learn it leads to a dead-end street and a wrecked life. Please, friends, steer clear of Sorek.

Samson was one of the biblical judges we read about in the Old Testament. In the book of Judges, God provides for us a record of the activity and action of the children of Israel during a very troubled time of their history. It was a day of spiritual upheaval and moral downfall. There are two phrases that best describe this time: "There was no King in Israel" and "every man did what was right in his own eyes" (17:6, 18:1, 19:1, 21:25). Honestly, it reminds me of today.

Samson is one of the best known of these judges but mostly for the wrong reasons. We do know that he was a man of faith, mentioned in Hebrews 11, but he was not necessarily faithful. Samson's conception, birth, and early years are most remarkable, some would say even miraculous. But once he reached puberty and adulthood, he was on a downward spiral. This man was likeable, but he was lustful. He was strong but also weak. His position was one of success, but his morals were those of failure. Samson was a he-man, but he had a she-problem.

Samson's lack of morals was his Achilles' heel. This term is well known from ancient Greek mythology. Achilles was a great warrior and hero of the Trojan War. Achilles was seemingly invincible, and there was a reason why. When he was a child, his mother Thetis, a sea goddess, held him by the heel and dipped him into the River Styx. Every part of his body was protected, except the heel by which he was held. That very small part was vulnerable. From this story, we have developed the term "Achilles' heel," which describes our greatest point of vulnerability. Achilles was struck by an arrow on this precise spot, and he died. For Samson, his Achilles heel was a *foreign female* (14:1), a *Gaza girl* (16:1–3), and a *Sorek sister* (16:4).

Everyone has an Achilles' heel of some type. It might be money or madness, anger or addiction. For Samson, it was his lust and lack of morals. And for the man whose name means brightness or sunshine, it was about to get very dark.

There is a little bit of Samson in everyone, especially men. This bad boy of the Bible battled lust, ignored counsel, disregarded boundaries, pushed the envelope, and broke the rules; he can't control his anger and seemingly never learns from his mistakes, so he is destined to repeat them. Surely, none of this describes you or me.

When you view the resume of Judge Samson, you find that many inconsistencies were present long before he traveled to Sorek and met Delilah. What were the things that stand out that soon brought him down?

Samson Refused Wise Counsel (14:1–3)

This young man was blessed with a godly set of parents who wanted the best for their amazing offspring. But he wanted to go to a distant land and retrieve a woman who was an enemy of Jehovah God;

this was an absolute no-no. In spite of their counsel and directive, Samson chose to go his own way and do his own thing.

I recall doing that many times in my teenage years. On one particular occasion, I needed to buy a car. I found the one I thought I would look best in and impress my peers the most. I overlooked the fact that it had high miles, a poor maintenance record, a rusted-out floor, and a dead battery before I test-drove it. My dad was not impressed with the car, the salesman, or me, and he voiced his reluctance. I bought the lemon, I mean car, anyway, and as you can imagine, it wasn't a wise decision.

Samson's disregard for his parents' counsel was much more serious and much more costly.

Samson Never Learned to Control His Emotions

Part of me wonders how this guy with the wandering eye and volcanic emotions ever became a judge, but he did. It's not just an issue that we fail and make poor choices; the bigger issue comes when we fail to learn from them and change.

Two of the leading areas Samson faced were his lust and his anger. Here was a guy who never learned to avert his eyes whenever he saw a woman. His look became lust, and it was an arrow straight to his heel *and his heart.* His anger was also noteworthy; he slew people, burned crops, and destroyed property, all out of anger.

Will Rogers once remarked, "People who fly off the handle seldom have a good landing." That's true. Adrian Rogers once said, "Be careful because anger is only one letter away from danger." That's good. Here is the bottom line: It's hard to save face when you keep losing your head.

Samson Violated God's Word (and His Vow)

There are multiple examples of this reality. He married outside God's commands, he touched a dead carcass, he went to improper places, he reacted in ungodly ways. In many ways, he lived a life contrary to God's Word and His will. Yes, according to Hebrews 11, he was an example of faith, but not of faithfulness. One example, Hebrews 11:32–34, is the only time we read something exemplary, and all it says is that once weak, he was made strong.

Samson Began to Treat the Things of God as Trivial (16:4–17)

When you read these verses of the Sorek seduction, it's quite obvious Samson is playing with fire. He shuns the Gaza harlot and leaves in a rage, only to wind up in Sorek: a bad choice again. Another city, another encounter, another arrow to the heel. Samson hangs around, lays around, fools around, and eventually caves. Here is the real issue: He didn't know where his strength lay. It wasn't in his hair; it was in his holiness. It was in his vow to Israel's God. And now, he didn't know his strength had left. He jumped up out of Delilah's lap as before, only to discover something was different; the touch of God had departed from him (16:20). The enemy seized him, shackled him, and shamed him. Remember, sin binds then blinds and ultimately grinds ever so fine. Such was true for Judge Sam.

Samson's Life Ends in Humiliation and Favor (16:22–30)

Verse 22 says of Samson, "However, the hair of his head began to grow again." God allows a restoration of sorts to happen to Samson, but it is short-lived. His strength returns if only for a moment and for a purpose. God uses this situation to ultimately accomplish His purpose. (Look back at 14:4.)

There is an interesting phrase Samson uses before his death: "Lord God, please remember me." It's very similar to what was uttered by the unnamed thief on the cross (Luke 23:42) and unfruitful Hannah, the wife of Elkanah (1 Samuel 1:11). Now we read of Samson. Put that all together. If you are lost like this thief, saved and burdened over an issue like Hannah, or a believer who has blown it, why not get things right today and ask God to remember you?

There is so much we can learn from Samson's life, mostly from his foolish choices and poor decisions. In that sense, don't be like Samson, and never travel to Sorek.

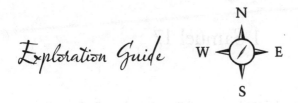

Exploration Guide

1. When you think of the book of Judges, what comes to your mind?
2. Samson is seen as a man of faith, but he wasn't always faithful. What are some examples of this? Is this ever true with you?
3. What is your Achilles' heel? How are you guarding against or overcoming this area?
4. Think of a time when you refused wise counsel. What was the outcome?
5. What lessons (good and bad) best stand out to you from Samson's life?
6. Is there a special situation you need God to remember on your behalf? Give it to Him today.

Valley of Elah

1 Samuel 17

Everybody loves the biblical story of David and Goliath (well, uh, except Goliath). Surely you are aware of the Philistine giant from Gath named Goliath and the really young shepherd boy named David. What you may not know is the name of the valley where they fought; it's the Valley of Elah.

The word *Elah* is a personal name of several people in the Old Testament, but it's better known as the location of David's victory. 1 Samuel 21:9 says David killed Goliath in the Valley of Elah. The word means oak, mighty tree, or terebinth (a rather large, sprawling tree native to this area).

The Valley of Elah is in Shephelah, some fourteen miles southwest of Jerusalem. Coursing through this valley is a small stream, or a wadi, as the Arabs call it. This streambed would fill and flow during the rainy season. In the bed of this wadi, you would (and can) find hundreds of small stones like the kind David used to kill Goliath.

Currently, on the top of the dresser in our bedroom are five smooth stones that my wife picked up when we were in Elah. Every morning as we awaken and dress for the day, we see these rocks and are reminded of this improbable victory. Or should I say, this amazing display of God's power.

When we hear today of someone throwing stones, it's usually in a negative or destructive capacity. A friend of mine wrote a song detailing how easy it is for followers of Jesus to pick up stones and prepare to attack.

But Elah was different. This valley is not a small or narrow ravine. In many ways, it's more like a small canyon. The ancient site was probably about a mile or so wide and even wider in spots. When our bus drove into the area, we were surrounded by mountains, and in this valley was a dry streambed; perhaps the very one David reached down into and chose his weapons. What a moment this was.

I quietly sat there and imagined; armies, Philistines, Goliath, Saul, David, rocks, and God. Sayings and sermons came to my mind:

"Many thought Goliath was too big to hit; David thought he was too big to miss."

"Your giant may not be as big as Goliath, but he is as bad."

"Goliath's height ... Israel's plight; David's fight ... God's might."

"The giants of your life may be just as horrible, hateful, and huge."

"David's foe, feud, faith, and fame."

"Your Goliath may be bigger than you, but he's smaller than God."

I'm sure as you read these words and think of this story, other sermons, illustrations, or situations come to mind. Even today, some three thousand-plus years later, we talk of "slaying the giants in our life" or a "David versus Goliath" matchup. You know the one, when the underdog gains the upper hand and comes out on top.

In my first book, *Big Doors Swing on Small Hinges*, I have a chapter entitled "But David." So instead of rehashing that idea, I want to point out several great truths I learned from this text (1 Samuel 17).

Why don't you stop reading for a moment and get your Bible? Turn to this text and slowly read through a story you know all too well. That might be our problem at times. The familiarity we have with a story, a text, or an idea can lull us into complacency. The adage says, "Familiarity breeds contempt." That means that one's extensive knowledge of some story or close association with someone can lead to a loss of respect and appreciation.

Have you faced any giants lately? You know, giant problems, giant concerns, giant struggles, giant debts, or giant obstacles. Maybe it's a larger-than-life need or a circumstance or situation that is so massive or problematic that a favorable outcome seems out of reach. Everyone on Israel's side of the valley felt this way; everyone except a young shepherd boy.

But David.

As you let this text marinate in your heart, take note of these twelve ideas:

- Goliaths are very big and quite intimidating (3–8).
- Fear has a way of paralyzing people (11).
- Different types of battles will come the believer's way daily (16).
- Most opponents and opportunities come in the normal routine of life (17–19).
- Some circumstances and needs are bigger (and more crucial) than our giants (26).
- There are times when our toughest battles are with those closest to us (28–30).
- The key to our success is not in who we are but in whom we serve (31–33).
- God uses previous and smaller issues to prepare us for current and larger ones (34–37).
- You can't fight your battles with someone else's armor (38–39).
- The Lord will supply you when necessary with the strength and source for victory (40–45).
- When God has spoken, we can run towards (and not from) our challenge (24, 48).
- God's ultimate goal has always been His own glory (46).

When all is said and done, David takes Goliath's sword and cuts off the giant's head. Look at verse 54: "Then David took the Philistine's head and brought it to Jerusalem, but he put his weapons in his tent." David drags that huge spear and that heavy sword into his own tent, as a reminder of what God can do. Perhaps he hung them next to the lion's skull and the bear's paw.

There is also a legend that says when David brought Goliath's head to Jerusalem, he buried it at a place called Golgotha, "the place of the skull." Of course, this is one of the names for the location of Jesus's death. That part of the story is just a legend, but the location is the place of our ultimate victory.

N

Exploration Guide   W ◄—◆—► E

S

1. Do you know any really tall people? How do you feel when you are around them?
2. What are the names of some of the giants you are currently facing (for example, fear, lust, pornography, addiction, etc.)?
3. Of the twelve ideas mentioned in this chapter, which stand out to you? Why?
4. David's previous battles had prepared him for his current one. What have you faced previously that you can look back to in your current need?
5. What are some of the weapons God has provided for us to come out victorious?

Mount Carmel

1 Kings 18

As a preacher of the Gospel, you can imagine that Mount Carmel is one of my favorite places to visit. Mount Carmel is the towering mountain range where the prophet Elijah confronted the prophets of Baal. This beautiful mountain range is in the north, not far from the Mediterranean Coast, overlooking the Jezreel Valley.

Elijah makes an interesting statement in 1 Kings 18:21 that is equally challenging today: "How long will you hesitate between two opinions? If the Lord is God, follow Him; but if Baal is [the real] God, follow him." Many people in our world today are still hesitating between opinions. Our world needs some Elijahs, and we need the fire of God to fall.

Baal is a pagan word for "lord." In Elijah's day, there were many different kinds of Baals. There would be Baals of knowledge, Baals for military ability, and Baals aiding one's health. There were even Baals in charge of people's prosperity and wealth. Many people of our day still serve this god.

However, the primary Baal was the god that controlled the rain. Oddly enough, this was the god of fertility, and *Carmel* means a fertile or fruitful field.

If you've been to the Holy Land during the late spring to early fall, you know how hot and dry it is. It is crucial that these rainy seasons come, and when they do, the locals see this as God's blessing and provision.

In Elijah's day, the nation was divided, and there was much

unrest. Israel was the name of the Northern region, and Judah was the Southern. Israel was led by wicked King Ahab and his worse-than-wicked wife, Jezebel. Ahab and Jezebel led this nation into rebellion against God; they embraced Baal worship.

It was thought that the rain Baal rested during the summer months, and thus there was no rain. In the fall, Baal would awaken and have sexual relations with the Asherah (the goddess), and then the rains would come. People in Elijah's day mimicked this practice and basically turned the Baal worship centers into houses of prostitution. No doubt, these pagan practices were contrary to God's law, handed down by Moses and shared by Elijah. In times of severe drought, the people even sacrificed their newborn children in an appeasement to their god so they might get some rain. Pagan. Ungodly. Demonic.

It was into this setting that God called Elijah to go and to preach. And Elijah was up to the challenge. (And you thought your field was tough or your church was sinful). Before you knew it, there was a showdown, and God's prophet called for His fire to come down.

As I scan the landscape of today's church, I must tell you, our greatest need is not man, money, might, machinery, or some new method. Our greatest need is for God's fire to fall, from the church house to the White House to your house and to my house.

It doesn't matter if you are a preacher or a professor, an elder or an educator, a CEO or an hourly employee; we all stand in need of God's fire to fall. In the early church, they enjoyed the enduement without all of the equipment; today, we have all the equipment, but we lack the enduement of power.

The Foolishness of Ahab

When you go back over this passage, it is so obvious what is happening. Elijah has thrown down a challenge, and pitiful King Ahab is helpless to respond. Look at it all: two oxen, two men, two altars, two gods, and two outcomes. Ahab's demise is summed up this way: "There was no voice, no one answered, and no one paid attention" (v. 29).

The Faith of Elijah

Elijah was a man of great faith and fervor. He was a preacher, but he was also a prayer. It is obvious to me what Elijah does; did you see it? He put God's name on the line, and he put his own name there too. Bottom line: Any God that can't burn wet wood is not worth much. Elijah wanted them to know that the God of Abraham, Isaac, and Jacob is the true God of Israel and that Elijah was His servant and did all these works at the Lord's leading.

Let me ask you, when was the last time you prayed with the faith and expectation of Elijah? Listen to his words: "Answer me, O God answer me, that these people may know that you O Lord are God" (v. 37). Something will happen when we pray like that.

The Fire of God

Scripture says that God's fire fell; the sacrifice was consumed. The wood, stones, dust, and water were all gone, and the onlookers' hearts were turned to the Lord.

When was the last time you really saw God's fire fall? See, the test of a great work of God is not fame, finances, figures, fellowship, or fanciness; it is fire. I read recently that when God's fire falls, sin is burned out, the Savior is burned in, and the self is burned up. To that, I say amen.

Exploration Guide   W ←⊕→ E (N / S)

1. Scan back through your Bible and view some of the many great stories of Elijah. Which is your favorite? Why?

2. Read 1 Kings 18:21. Are there areas in your life that you've struggled with or refuse to give to the Lord? Why do you think this is?

3. Is there a current prayer need in your life you need God to come through on? Have you prayed with earnestness, as the prophet did? If not, will you?

4. Elijah was a great preacher and prayer, but he still faced battles and had enemies (for example, chapter 19). Why not stop and pray for your pastor right now?

5. What are some practical ways I can encourage my pastor and church staff?

Valley of Beracah

2 Chronicles 20

There are times in each of our lives when the report comes back less than promising, and it seems to provide more questions than answers. For example, a family is anxiously awaiting the report on a loved one's tumor. Or your company is about to expand, but the cost estimates are way too high. Maybe it's a bid you submitted for a project you really desired. Events like these happen to someone every single day. In many situations, the report back is favorable and positive. Sadly, in many cases, it's not what you wanted to hear.

What do you do or how do you respond when fear is in your future, hardship is on the horizon, or difficulty is at the end of your day?

I recall when Michelle and I decided that I would retire from the pastorate and become the president of Friends of Nazareth. A key piece of our puzzle going forward would be the sale of our home. Granted, we built our dream home, never intending to leave; I was only leaving by rapture, not resignation. God had other plans.

When we met with a real estate agent, she began to paint for us a not-so-pretty picture. Because of the local economy, area demographics, size of home, price, and other variables, the average time needed to sell a home like ours was in excess of two years. Ouch. That was not what we wanted to hear.

Many questions began to fill my heart and mind. Are we out of God's will? Have we missed the Lord? Have we overbuilt for our area? (Note: My agent was so right. As I pen these words, our house has been on the market for two years and still no contract. Do you need

54

a house in Scottsboro, Alabama? As Alexander Shunnarah would say, "Call me Alabama.")

One day, such a report came to Jehoshaphat, the king of Judah. A trans-Jordan coalition of Amorites, Moabites, and Edomites was coming up to fight the king and to destroy his kingdom. Not only was the enemy coming, they were close. Recent suggestions have equated this valley with the Kidron Valley, near Jerusalem. However, better evidence places it toward the Salt (Dead) Sea in the wilderness. Today, it's called Wadi Bereikut.

When news comes, the enemy is already in En Gedi. If you've been to Israel and journeyed to the Dead Sea for a swim, you probably stopped off in En Gedi. It's like an oasis in the midst of the desert: a waterfall, swimming hole, palm trees, and gazelles. No wonder the army camped there.

Before you read more, why not stop and refresh yourself with this story in 2 Chronicles 20? Some call this chapter the process of praise, the roadmap to blessing, or the steps through a mess. Whatever you call it, it is no doubt a story worth reading and knowing.

What would be the king's response to such a situation, and what should be ours when the news is not good and the circumstances are not promising?

Wait on the Lord (1–13)

After his wicked alliance with King Ahab of Israel and the improper report of many false prophets, God had finally gotten Jehoshaphat's attention and returned him to safety. Jehu rebukes the king, and positive changes seem to be coming. It's after this that we encounter the ordeal in our text.

Still, an enemy is coming from beyond the Jordan, and Jehoshaphat's heart is filled with fear. The king then does a wise thing: "he turned his attention to seek the Lord ... he calls for a fast ... and he prays" (vv. 3–6). Isn't it amazing how when God gets our attention and we respond favorably, good things normally happen?

King Jehoshaphat's prayer is worth noting and learning from, it really is one of the great prayers of the Bible. In it, he reminds God what the Lord said and did, and he confesses his own inability. Listen to these words: "O our God, will you not judge them? For we are powerless before this great multitude who are coming against us; nor do we know what to do, but our eyes are on you." And they waited before the Lord. (Incidentally, God would rather you go through a defeat that leaves you humble than a victory that leaves you proud.)

Listen for God's Word (14–17)

When we get ourselves in a position like the king, God will speak. God had His prophet near and ready, and the Word of the Lord came through Jahaziel. His sermon basically had two points: You need not *fear*, and you need not *fight*. See, the same God Who can handle your fears can take care of your foes. By the way, most of the things that cause our hearts to fear never come about; God tells us again and again in His Word to not fear.

Before you get too excited about a sermon with only two points, there were a couple of subpoints. God tells the king where he is to go and what he is to do. What courage this must have given the king; the Lord was with him (v. 17).

(A side note: I'm often asked how many points are needed in a good sermon; at least one!)

Learn to Worship

What happens next in our story is not only marvelous; it is miraculous. Picture this: King Jehoshaphat gathers the musicians and choirs, and he stations them between the two armies. (I imagine that's where many worship pastors feel they have been positioned: between the contemporary and the traditional armies). "When they began singing and praising … [the enemy was] routed" (v. 22). Some of the words used in the text are interesting:

"who sang" (21): *Yadah*, to worship with extended hands

"who praised" (21): *hallal,* to laud, boast or to celebrate; to become clamorously foolish

"when singing" (22): *rinnah,* to shout a word of joy or praise, to sing with outstretched arms

"and praising" (22): *tehillah,* the singing of hallals, songs of praise

"there they blessed the Lord" (26) *barak,* to kneel, to bless, to praise the Lord

Are you beginning to understand? Do you get the picture? God not only commands and likes our praise; He uses it and responds to it. Surely the psalmist had something like this in mind when He penned these words:

> For the Lord takes pleasure in His people;
> He will beautify the afflicted ones with salvation.
> Let the godly ones exult in glory;
> Let them sing for joy on their beds.
> Let the high praises of God be in their mouth,
> And a two-edged sword in their hand,
> To execute vengeance on the nations
> And punishment on the peoples,
> To bind their kings with chains
> And their nobles with fetters of iron,
> To execute on them the judgment written;
> This is an honor for all His godly ones. (Psalm 149:4–9)

It saddens me how so many people today seem to resist a glorious service of praise and worship when God has designed this activity to stop the enemy dead in his tracks.

The Welfare That Resulted (24–30)

Much could be said about the result of such a service or what God does when we worship. Two things seem to stand out: God blessed them with *prosperity.* Please don't think I'm one of "those kinds of preachers" or that I'm encouraging a prosperity theology; I'm not. However, I am saying (loudly) that God wants His people to be blessed and to be a blessing. It was so true here that they named the place where all this happened the Valley of Beracah: the valley of blessing.

God blessed them with *peace*. This might just be the greater of the two provisions. For you see, when all of your substance is gone, if you still have serenity, you are blessed. Wouldn't it be great if our churches and communities and countries could know this peace "on all sides" (v. 30)?

Watch out.

I wish that was all there was to the story of Judah's king. However, there's a "however" (v. 33). There are two events that are like bookends in the life of Jehoshaphat; one is his alliances and one his allegiances. He allied himself with wicked men like Ahab (ch. 13) and Ahaziah (ch. 20), and he would not remove the high places (pagan altars), which proved their hearts were not right with God (v. 33).

Friends, please hear me say, praises in your mouth or accomplishments on your resume do not rule out disobedience in your heart. Lessons are many in scripture, both good and bad.

Exploration Guide

N
W ⊕ E
S

1. Recall a time when a report came back to you that wasn't what you wanted to hear. How did that make you feel? What was your response?
2. Many of Jehoshaphat's troubles stemmed from his wicked alliance with King Ahab. Think of a time when you made a poor decision, and it proved difficult.
3. What aspects of the king's prayer most stick out to you?
4. Is there a situation in your life, marriage, church, family, or job that may require you to fast in addition to praying? What does God's Word teach about fasting?

5. Which of the words for our praise/worship most speak to you or describe you?

6. How is the phrase "God blessed them with prosperity" different from the prosperity Gospel many embrace today?

Valley of Shadows

Psalm 23

Today's text is perhaps the most quoted and familiar in all of the Old Testament, if not the entire Bible. It has been shared at devotions and at decorations. We read it at graduation ceremonies and on battlefields. Mostly, we reserve it for funerals. And, yes, as a pastor, I've been guilty many times over.

There is something about funerals and death that has a way of messing us up. My maternal grandfather was a funeral director and a funeral homeowner. In fact, he even sold funeral clothes, better known as burial garments. I never understood the need; why not just wear what you have? Oh, well, it did put food on the table and bought my Christmas gifts. My mother has often spoken of growing up in the funeral home and seeing "draped bodies" and a "bloody pond." I know she was young and still in school, but I would have considered moving out on my own.

Death is a subject we all seek to avoid. We may even squirm or cringe when we think of it. However, the Bible talks about how our Lord and our faith in His promises can take the fear out of the funeral and the grief out of the grave. Listen to the writer of Hebrews: "He himself [Jesus] likewise also partook of the same, that through death He might render powerless him who had the power of death, that is, the devil, and might free those who through fear of death were subject to slavery all their lives" (Hebrews 2:14–15). An improper understanding of death is like a chain that enslaves you; it frightens you. All of us at times have had to wrestle with these feelings. Can I just tell you this: You are really not ready to live until you are no longer afraid to die.

For all of us, death is an appointment. "It is appointed unto man once to die" (Hebrews 9:27), and to those who have met our Lord, it is an advancement. For "to live is Christ and to die is gain" (Philippians 1:21).

David was the writer of this famed psalm, and don't forget his job as a young man: He tended his family's sheep. He was a shepherd. This psalm reminds us that what David did for his sheep, our Lord, the Good Shepherd, will do for us. One of David's jobs was to transport his sheep from the lowlands to the high plains. To get from one area to the other required the shepherd to lead his sheep through a wadi: the bed of a stream that was dry except during the rainy seasons. The location David knew is called Wadi Qelt.

The Wadi Qelt, named Nahal Prat in Hebrew, is located today in the West Bank. It originates near Jerusalem and runs down into the Jordan River Valley, near Jericho. It ultimately flows into the Dead Sea. This area has a unique variety of flowers, grass, and vegetation. The gorge begins at 2,700 feet above sea level and descends to the lowest spot on the earth, the Dead Sea, at 1,300 feet below sea level. It's like a miniature Grand Canyon, and in some places, it's very narrow. Even at the height of the sun, it was full of shadows. Animals, lepers, and robbers would hide out in the crevices and caves of this wadi. Shepherds called this the Valley of the Shadows, and David knew it well.

In the same way David used this valley to bring his flock from the lowlands into the mountains for pasture, God uses death to transport His children to their eternal home. I can't help but think of the words of the old hymn, "Higher Ground":

I'm pressing on the upward way
new heights I'm gaining every day.
Still praying as I onward bound
Lord plant my feet on higher ground.

But dear friend, this psalm is not just soaked with tears from a funeral; it is filled with theology for our faith. It's not merely about a God Who is with you in death; it is about a Lord Who guides and protects you in life. It's a writing worth noting and knowing.

As we think about this particular valley, let's hang our thoughts on four hooks: land, light, lesson, and Lord.

The Land

When you know something about geography, you come to understand that it is impossible to have a valley without surrounding mountains. I currently live in Scottsboro, Alabama, in what is called the Tennessee Valley. This city is bordered by what locals call Skyline Mountain and Sand Mountain. The valley is made because of the surrounding mountains.

Psalm 23 is called a valley psalm; it is surrounded by two mountains. In Psalm 22, we read about the blood-stained slopes of Mount Calvary, and in Psalm 24, we learn of the sunlit peaks of Mount Zion. When you put this trinity of psalms together, you see our Lord dying, living, and coming again. It's one of the sweet joys of God's Word.

Reader, the Christian life is not all sunshine and laughter. There will be seasons of sorrow and days of difficulty. When you're in such a valley, remember David's words: "Yea, though I walk through the valley." You aren't staying there.

The Light

David called this a valley of shadows. In the same way you can't have valleys without mountains, you can't have shadows without light. It's so easy for us to focus on the shadows when we should look to the light. But shadows are harmless. The shadow of a car can't strike, the shadow of a dog can't bite, and the shadow of a tree can't crush. When you are in a moment of shadows, look for light.

Preachers often tell the story of Pastor Donald G. Barnhouse after the untimely death of his young wife. As the family was traveling to the burial, the afternoon sun cast a long shadow of a truck on a neighboring building. Instantly, the wise pastor saw it as a teaching moment for his confused children. "Do you see that shadow and that truck? Which had you rather run over Mama?"

"The shadow, Daddy," they said. "It wouldn't hurt."

"Exactly," he said. "This week, the shadow hit your mama; the truck hit Jesus two thousand years ago." Don't ever forget that.

The Lesson

David writes of fearing "evil." Yes, this valley was dark, dangerous, and often difficult. But we wouldn't even know about evil if there weren't also good. It's so easy to focus on all the bad things and bad people of our day; sadly, we act as if sin is superior. Folks, our Lord, not sin, is sovereign. No one or no thing is greater than our God. "Greater is He that is in me than he that is in this world" (1 John 4:4).

The Lord

What benefit is a good shepherd if he is not with you in the difficult moments of life? As a child of the great God, you will never know a time without the Lord's presence. See, Jesus was forsaken by His Father so you never would be. In fact, He said, "I'll never leave you nor forsake you" (Hebrews 13:5). Listen to some verses from another of David's great psalms:

Where can I go from Your Spirit?
Or where can I flee from Your presence?
If I ascend to heaven, You are there;
If I make my bed in Sheol, behold, You are there.
If I take the wings of the dawn,
If I dwell in the remotest part of the sea,
Even there Your hand will lead me,
And Your right hand will lay hold of me.
If I say, "Surely the darkness will overwhelm me,
And the light around me will be night,"
Even the darkness is not dark to You,

And the night is as bright as the day.
Darkness and light are alike to You. (Psalm 139:7–12)

In the moment of our death, our Lord is not there necessarily to discipline us but rather to defend us. With His rod and staff, I can imagine Moses and the children of Israel. With the rod, he held off Pharaoh's approaching army, and with the staff, he led them through the Red Sea. God is my defender and my deliverer, and through death, He is taking me to higher ground.

"Precious in the sight of the Lord is the death of His saints" (Psalm 116:15).

Exploration Guide

1. When was the last time you recall hearing Psalm 23? Was it at a funeral or a sermon?
2. What does death mean to you? Do you fear dying?
3. How is death an appointment?
4. Read Psalms 22, 23, and 24 together. Did you see the valley and the mountains?
5. What is the difference in our Lord being the Good, Great, and Chief Shepherd? What do each of these imply?
6. Paul said, "To die is gain." How is this so?

Valley of Sin (Sorrows)

Psalm 32

When I'm looking to learn something, I generally choose learning from a veteran, not a rookie; someone with years of experience, not a novice. In saying that, there is so much we can learn from David, some good and some, well, not so good.

David was a great *singer*. He is called the "sweet psalmist of Israel," and it's easy to picture him out with his sheep, singing away. David was a great *songwriter*. In fact, the psalms are part of the Hebrew hymnbook. It's good to sing the Word. David was a great *saint*. He is a flock leader, giant slayer, and a man after the heart of God. Perfect? No. Made right? Absolutely. David was a great *sovereign*, like Saul and Solomon. David reigned for forty years in one of Israel's highest and most prosperous times. They called it Israel's "Golden Age."

Yes, each of these terms is true of David. Indeed, he was a great singer, songwriter, saint, and sovereign, but David was also a great *sinner*. There are many recorded times in David's life that reveal his disobedience and his utter depravity. One of those scenes involves his committing adultery with Bathsheba and trying to cover it up by having her husband Uriah killed. Adultery and murder. As I said, David was indeed a great sinner.

Surely you know this story and the outcome (2 Samuel 11, 12). Following his confrontation with Nathan, we learn about David's contrition in Psalm 51. My Bible adds this heading before the chapter begins: "A Psalm of David, when Nathan the prophet came to him, after he [David] had gone in to Bathsheba." Psalm 51 is David's plea for forgiveness. Psalm 32 is a record to the fact that confession is made, forgiveness is granted, and restoration is complete.

In Psalm 51, David replies, "God, if you'll forgive and restore me, I'll learn from it, change my ways, and even teach others" (my paraphrase). In Psalm 32, David has left the bedroom and gone to the classroom. He is now "teaching transgressors Your [God's] ways" (51:13a). All of us are transgressors, and we can learn something from this "seasoned sinner."

In Psalm 32, David has been in a Valley of Sin (Sorrow), and he is on his way out. He who descended into this self-made valley is now ascending. The valley of Psalms 51 and 32 is not a literal one, geographically speaking, but it is real, nonetheless. See, though David's body may have been in the palace, his heart was in the pit.

Psalm 32 is called a "Maskil." This word means to "give instruction or to help in understanding." Here, David is offering some help for his readers, then and now. There are great truths all of us can learn from David's battle and defeat. Goliath may have been his tallest foe, but Bathsheba was his toughest. (There is a difference between an armor-clad soldier and a beautiful naked woman.)

You Can Be Forgiven (1)

The testimony of David and many other personalities of scripture is this: You can be forgiven. Peter denied the Lord, Paul was the chief of sinners, and John Mark walked off from his calling. But forgiveness was granted to each, and total restoration came.

Personally, my life before Christ was marred and scarred with sin. What a great sinner I too was (and am). Perhaps that's why I so love the words

Amazing Grace how sweet the sound
That saved a wretch like me
I once was lost but now I'm found
Was blind but now I see.

I'm sure you can say and sing the same. Or, you may need this understanding, this forgiveness. It doesn't matter what you've done or are doing; God's offer of forgiveness is available. You can be forgiven.

Sin Has Many Faces and Features (1–2)

Sin is an offense to God, and it is so radical that the Holy Spirit uses many words and ideas to describe it. There are as many as fifteen different Hebrew words for "sin," and in Psalm 32, David uses four of them. *Transgression* means to get out of line or out of bounds. It implies rebellion and a revolt against authority. *Sin* is to miss the mark or to fall short. Something is missing in our life, and we've come up way short of God's standard. *Iniquity* means we are utterly evil, wicked, bent, and crooked. Every human heart is affected and perverted. *Deceit* (or *guilt*) means exactly what it says. We are insincere, cunning, hateful, and hurtful. Sin is more than just what we do; it's who we are. We are not sinners because we sin; we sin because we are sinners. David had finally come to see this and to understand it, and now he wants to help others see it too.

Concealing Sin Is Never Wise (3–4)

For the better part of a year, King David had gone about his daily routine, perhaps thinking he had gotten away with something. One wonders if, every time he saw someone whispering or came upon a conversation, he thought, *I wonder if they know? Were they discussing me?*

Proverbs 28:13 reminds us, "He who conceals his transgressions will not prosper." This reminds me of what Joshua saw when, after his army had overtaken Jericho, Achan had taken some things that were banned. Later, when they came upon little Ai, they were utterly shamed. Achan had hidden items under his tent; Joshua didn't know, but God did. Unconfessed sin does the same. It will lead to defeat and render you ineffective.

Confession Is Always Worthwhile (5–7a)

Solomon reminds us, "He who confesses his sins and forsakes them will find compassion" (Proverbs 28:13b). John tells us, "If we confess our sins, He is faithful and just to forgive us of our sins and to cleanse us from all unrighteousness" (1 John 1:9). James adds, "Therefore, confess your sins to one another … that you may be healed" (5:16). The confession will lead one from the pit of despair to the heights of deliverance.

I love the reminder given by Christian pastor, author, and apologist, John Blanchard:

What man covers
God will uncover
And, what man uncovers
God will cover.

God Will Restore Your Lost Joy (7)

When David first confessed his sins in Psalm 51, he stated, "Restore to me the joy of thy salvation." David had lost his joy, his song. Imagine that; the great singer was no longer singing, and the great songwriter could no longer pen songs. Now his song is back.

You are my hiding place.

You preserve me from trouble.

You surround me with songs of deliverance.

God is the great remover and restorer. He will remove your sin and guilt, and He will restore your song and joy. When you give God your sin, He'll give you His song.

It's time to think this thing over. Are you out of fellowship with God (or someone else)? Are you carrying a grudge? Is there a secret sin you've held onto or maybe some unresolved conflict with a family member, neighbor, or coworker?

Three times in Psalm 32, David uses the word *Selah*. This word is thought by many to have been a musical pause, a built-in stop to make readers look, listen, and ponder what's being said. David writes about his conviction of sin and how it emotionally and physically affected him; selah. Then he speaks of confession. "I will no longer hide my sin ... I will confess ... you forgave ... my guilt is gone. Selah." Then David utters with great confidence, "You are my hiding place; you keep me from trouble [and trouble from me]. You alone provide joy. Selah."

Author and preacher John Phillips is now in heaven. I once heard him say that "Selah" was God's break to say, "There ... what do you think about that?" After David leaves the pit of despair and comes out on the other side, Psalm 32 is his exhortation and reminder to all others, "There, what do you think about that?" Selah.

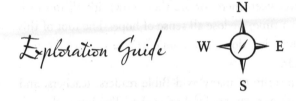

Exploration Guide

1. Which of these descriptions of David best stands out to you and why: singer, songwriter, saint, shepherd, sovereign?
2. David was a man "after God's heart." If he was such a depraved sinner, what does that teach us? How can this be a challenge?
3. Have you ever had to confront someone for their sin (as Nathan did David) or be confronted? How did this make you feel?
4. Have you ever been guilty of hiding a sin?
5. Go back and reread the words of John Blanchard. How does this speak to you?
6. Sin has a way of robbing our joy. Can you think of an occasion when this was true for you?

Valley of Despair

Psalm 34

The Valley of Despair is not a literal place, but it's not mythical, either. In fact, if you've ever been there (or are there now), it's all too real. When we face such a time, we lose all sense of hope. The root of this word means literally to be "down from hope." Have you ever been in the Valley of Despair?

Psalm 34 is a favorite of many avid Bible readers, teachers, and preachers. Perhaps it's one you are fond of as well. The ironic thing is that few people are aware of the background of this writing. What led David to write what he did? Why was he so desperate?

Let me give you a bit of background. After David defeated Goliath, he immediately achieved rock star status. Everyone was talking about David's courage and his conquest, defeating the giant of Gath. After David killed the Philistine, the scripture says the women came out of all the cities to celebrate. King Saul came with his entourage, including young David. The women began to chant, "Saul has killed his thousands, but David his tens of thousands" (1 Samuel 18:7).

In that very moment, Saul felt threatened; he was bitter and upset. From that moment, the king began to view David with suspicion and looked for ways to kill him.

After several close calls and near-misses, David decided to flee. Young David hid in one location and then another; he moved from cave to cave. He was in the wilderness near the Dead Sea: not a luxurious place to hang out.

David survived for a while, but his body and soul were growing weary. And then he made a crucial mistake; he went west to the land of the Philistines, the enemy. Let me be very forthright and say we are never safe or right when we're out of God's will.

Things appeared okay for a brief time, but then it was determined who this David was. Ultimately, David ended up lying, disguised his sanity, and finally escaped (1 Samuel 21:1–22:1). Perhaps he returned to the wilderness of Israel to hide. One can imagine this young man propped up in a cave and thinking back over all he had done and all God had done. "I should have never left; I should have trusted God."

From this stressful time and with his own disobedience in mind, David penned Psalm 34. In it, David learned about himself, his life, and his great God. And because he wrote this psalm, we can learn that too.

David pointed to several things that led to his despair. He wrote of *fearful circumstances* (4), *financial pressures* (6), and *foolish people* (16). (When I say financial pressures, maybe it's not a lack of money but of might; your bank account is not depleted, but your heart is.)

If we're all honest, each of those things has a way of making us feel hopeless at times. You know, when your business closes down and you no longer have a job; you are faced with more month (or mortgage) than money; or your toxic boss or family member has pushed you to the limit. In many ways, that was where David was (or at least where he had been). After he thought back over this scenario, he penned one of the great psalms (granted, none of them are bad).

What did David learn in the cave, in the wilderness, and in the enemies' camp? Let me list for you several truths; I encourage you to go back over each of these in your heart.

God Will Speak (4)

David said, "I sought the Lord and He answered." In other words, David was asking, seeking, and knocking (Matthew 7:7). I should hasten to say, we don't have to wait for God to speak; God has spoken, and we have His Word. I've learned that God uses His Word, prayer, circumstances, and people to reveal His will to us. Know this, God's will won't differ from His Word.

God Is Good (8)

When I was younger, there was a commercial on TV for Alka-Seltzer. The catch line said, "Try it, you'll like it." In verse 8, David is saying the same: I tried the Lord, and He is good; you should try His way too. The psalmist goes on to say, "If you need a refuge or some resources, look to the Lord—for He is good." Friends, I concur. God is good all the time, and all the time God is good.

God Is Always Aware (15–16)

When Joseph was in the pit, when Daniel was in the lions' den, when Jonah was sloshing around in the belly of the whale: At all times, God knew what was happening. And when David was in the wilderness, the cave, and the enemy palace, He was aware. The Lord knows where you are and what you're facing. To emphasize that, David says God's eyes and ears and face are all in play. Theologians would call that an anthropomorphism, when God is spoken of in human terms or characteristics. Whatever all of that means, isn't it good to know we have a God Who is personally vested in our lives? Amen.

God Is Near (18)

Earlier in this psalm, we are told that "the angel of the Lord encamps around those who fear Him" (7), and now we are told He is "near." For me, that creates confidence, joy, and peace. I read some time ago that we should take His nearness as personally as we do our pain; that's good. Let it sink in.

God Is Faithful (19–20)

David makes two bold statements in verse 19; don't miss either of them. Righteous people will have many afflictions, and God will help them through them all. To prove the faithfulness of God, the Holy Spirit leaps forward hundreds of years to give us an illustration. He reminds us that when Jesus is crucified, none of His bones were broken, and they weren't (John 19:33, 36). God has been and always will be faithful. In the same way He looked after Jesus, Jesus will look after you.

God Gets the Last Word (21–22)

It's so easy to get discouraged and feel despair in our world. When right is called wrong and wrong is called right, when the godly suffer and the ungodly prosper, when churches are closing and pot shops are thriving, it's easy to feel defeated. But God will have the final say; He will get the last word. God will slay the wicked, judge the ungodly, and rescue His own. All because of Jesus; my friend, you, if you know Him, will come out on top. The world is loud, but God gets the last word.

God Is Worthy of Worship (1–3)

Circle back with me, will you? As David thinks back over all he saw, all he learned, and all he now knows, his heart erupted in praise: "I will bless the Lord, I will not stop, everyone needs to hear this. When you see and hear this, you'll join me in praise" (1–3).

Now, our messed-up world, and many messed-up churches, will tell you that you'll only feel that way when you're healthy and wealthy, protected and prosperous. Not David. He learned all of this during times of fear (4), trouble (6), a broken heart (18a), a crushed spirit (18b), and much affliction (19).

Feelings of despair and moments of desperation come to all of us. It might be in a child's rebellion, a workplace crisis, or when your spouse admits to an affair. It can be physical, mental, emotional, relational, or spiritual. Despair is no respecter of persons.

This morning, I read a report of a young mother in my city who is evidently in the final stages of life. Her husband is confused, her children are scared, and her parents and friends are less than optimistic. All are watching, waiting, and I'm sure wondering what will come of her. I think this qualifies as despair.

When you're in the Valley of Despair, learn what David learned and shared in Psalm 34.

1. Why is jealousy such a problem for many? Do you struggle with this vice?

2. In Psalm 34, David recounts a season of rebellion when he was out of God's will. Can you recall a time like that for you? How did it make you feel? How was it resolved?

3. Think of a season you were in that felt hopeless. What led to this reaction?

4. Look back over the seven descriptions of God. Which is most needed by you today? Why?

5. Psalm 34 contains one of the many prophecies of Jesus's death. What are some others?

6. Who do you know that is currently in the Valley of Despair? How can you personally reach out to them and minister to them?

Valley of Baca

Psalm 84

Crying and tears are an amazing thing. Have you had a good cry lately? Or maybe I should ask, What is it that causes you to cry? It may be the result of a family dispute, a time of intense sorrow, or a fit of anger or rage. Tears may flow after a disappointing loss or a dramatic victory. Times of bereavement and joy have been known to produce tears. It seems the older I get, the more frequently I tend to cry; I'm just a big sissy.

I read recently of a biochemist who said that weeping has served humans for years as a way to relieve stress. The chemical makeup of emotional tears is different from the fake tears produced when we peel an onion. Emotional tears contain more of the body's toxins, whereas tears produced by onions are 98 percent water. Interesting.

Even the way men and women cry is different. Though there is no noticeable difference in the duration of crying episodes of men and women, they do cry differently. Men usually cry quietly, and their eyes brim neatly with tears. Women's cries are accompanied with other noises, and tears flow down their cheeks. (If the crier is a young girl, her episode may include a slammed door and a scream. That was not in the study; it was just inserted by the author.) Men cry on average 1.4 times per month, where women will cry about 5.3 times, with gusts up to 15.

So you don't get the idea that I'm picking on ladies, I recall a time a few years ago where I cried and cried over a situation within my family. It was the cry of a broken heart. When I finally regained my composure, my eyes were swollen, my face was stained, and my whole body hurt. I was not a pretty sight.

It might help us to know that a good cry has health benefits. Tears are secreted through a duct, much like sweat flows from your body's glands. When emotional tears flow, they aid your body by removing waste products and toxic substances. That's one reason people say they feel better after a good cry.

Dr. Alan Wolfelt, professor at the University of Colorado Medical School and Director of the Center for Loss and Life Transition, wrote in his book *Understanding Your Grief* (Companion Press, 2004), "I've even noticed physical changes in one following a time of tears. Not only do people feel better, they also look better." I would add if you are overcome with a sense of ugliness, go on and have a good cry. It may help you and us.

The psalmist had an interesting word he used for these moments of this feeling; it's the word *Baca*, which means adversity, weeping, or even balsam tree (because those trees exude a gum that makes it look as if the tree is crying). Some interpreters think it refers to the final stage of travel from Northern Palestine to Jerusalem. This area is named Ain el-Haramijeh. The name means a gloomy, narrow valley where brackish water trickles out of the rocks. These crying rocks are called the Valley of Baca.

When David uses the word in Psalm 84, it reflects a poetic play on words, and it describes the time when we endure hardship and weeping. The literal Valley of Baca is miles away from most of my readers; you may never travel there. But the spiritual idea is all too familiar, and we've all journeyed there.

If you haven't, you will.

Before I suggest how you can survive this valley, let me begin by saying that these are *ordinary seasons*. We know that God is sovereign, and He orchestrates our steps. He is also our Creator, and He designed us with tear ducts. Abraham wept over Sarah. Jacob wept over Joseph. David wept over Absalom. The widows wept over Dorcas. And Jesus wept over Lazarus and Jerusalem.

There are also *temporary seasons*. In Psalm 30:5, we read, "Weeping may last for the night, but a shout of joy will come in the morning." Isaiah 25:8 says that God "will wipe their tears from their faces." And in Revelation 7:17, we read, "And God shall wipe away every tear from their eyes."

So how do we make it through one of these seasons? How do we survive a Valley of Baca? The answer is found in Psalm 84. (Take a moment and read the twelve verses of this psalm).

Personal Worship (1–2)

Our worship is always crucial but especially in moments of hardship and seasons of trouble. Why? Because worship is a transfer of focus; it is a shifting of one's attention. In worship, my focus is no longer on myself or my situation; it's on my Lord. In this way, my worry can become worship, my pain can become praise, and my agony can result in adoration. Worship is not just a weekly service we attend; it is a daily practice of a growing and hurting believer.

Association with God's House and His People (3–4)

When difficult times come, don't run from God's house; run to it. An observation I made as a pastor through years of ministry; many hurting people in the world run to the church, while many bitter people in the church resort to the world. Strange, isn't it?

The psalmist said, "The bird has found a house and the swallow a nest," and God's people need a house too. And you have one; it's your local church. God's church is a place of blessing and praising (v. 4). Selah. Think about that.

Rely on God's Strength, Not Your Own (5, 7, 12)

One of the many things God teaches us in these moments is to learn to trust Him and rely on His strength. Solomon said, "Do not lean on your own understanding" (Proverbs 3:5–6). John the Baptist said, "He must increase, but I must decrease" (John 3:30).

This chapter reminds us that God's strength will aid our journey (v. 5), will increase and grow (v. 7), and will result in blessings (v.

12). I'm reminded of the line from the great old hymn "Great Is Thy Faithfulness": "strength for today and bright hope for tomorrow." Grant it, Lord.

An Active Prayer Life (8)

Can I just tell you: I'm no expert in the school of prayer. I'm still a student, but my, do I want to learn. Let me say this: If Jesus began His day with prayer (Mark 1:35), if He prayed over crucial decisions (Luke 6:12–13), if He prayed during tough times (Matthew 26:39), and if He ever lives to pray for us (John 8:34), what makes you think you can survive life (or your Baca) without it?

Lean on God's Provision (10–11)

In these two verses, David takes us to the classroom for some instruction, and he shows us several things:

- God's economy and timing is different from ours (v. 10).
- God's provision includes my direction "a sun" and my protection "a shield" (v. 11a).
- God's manner of blessing includes grace, for now, and glory for later (v. 11b).

Now, stop for a moment and ponder each of these realities. Ummm, that's good.

When You Face Your Baca, Dig a Well for Others (6)

When you pass through this valley, David said to "make it a spring" ... it "blesses." When we get to that level of understanding and maturity, God can use us to encourage others in their own setbacks.

I first heard that idea years ago from a friend named Lisa. Lisa married Matt, her college sweetheart, after they graduated from Clemson. They were in their early twenties, but soon after their wedding, Matt was diagnosed with cancer and died. Wait; that doesn't happen to young couples in their twenties who love Jesus passionately. Does it? Sometimes, it does, and it did to Matt and Lisa.

Lisa chronicled her amazing story in a book called *Love, Lisa*. When I invited her to address a women's group at our church, she spoke from Psalm 84:6, about the Valley of Baca. Honestly, I was the pastor and knew very little of her subject. Lisa challenged our ladies and me. When you go through these seasons, or face these moments, be intentional in "digging a well" so you can help other people who come after you.

People, God never wastes a hurt. When you are in this season, learn what He wants to teach you so you can dig a well and, in so doing, teach others.

All of this together tells me that crying can be healthy. Crying has a purpose. It's okay to have a good cry every now and then. And God can transform your Baca into a blessing.

Exploration Guide

N
W ✦ E
S

1. Do you recall the last time you had a good cry? What was it over?
2. It may be hard to worship during a Baca season, but it is necessary and worthwhile. Why is that?
3. Are you an active member of a local church? How has the church been used to minister to people in times of difficulty?
4. What does it mean to pray through? Do you recall an occasion when you or another did that?
5. Read vv. 10–11. Ponder for a moment these truths. What do they mean?
6. Is there a situation from your past God brought you through that could be a well for someone else? How can you make this known?

Valley of Dry Bones

Ezekiel 37

Of all the mountains and valleys we will examine in this book, perhaps none are more interesting or peculiar as this one. You might even say it's unbelievable. The story sounds like something you would glance at while waiting to check out at your local grocery store, but it is a truthful part of God's Word.

Perhaps the only thing more interesting than the story of these dry bones is the guy who saw them and wrote about it. Ezekiel was ministering to a difficult group of people at a difficult time. Sure, he was a fiery prophet (chapter 4), but he did some strange things. He at times slept on his right side and at times on his left (chapter 5). He shaved his head and face with a sharp sword (chapter 5). Once he cut his hair, he put it in three piles; one pile was burned, one pile was struck with the sword, and one pile was thrown to the wind. Were this guy on the scene today, we would have surely called him strange (ministry and people can drive you to do weird things).

Perhaps the only thing stranger than Ezekiel are the ways this vision of dry bones has been interpreted and preached. Some of these sermons and interpretations need to be burned, struck with a sword, or cast to the wind!

This prophecy is not about bodily resurrection, Replacement Theology, dead church services, or even revival. It's not about Mormonism and Joseph Smith. This prophecy is about Israel's rebirth, how it will come to pass, and what will be the result.

It's worth noting that Bible hermeneutics (the study of learning the proper interpretation) is a crucial science. The text means what it meant. That is, it means what it was intended to mean in its original context, as set forth by the author. There may be multiple applications, but there is only one interpretation. Don't overlook this point in Ezekiel 37.

God's chosen people seemed to be helpless and hopeless. History tells us that Israel was invaded in 605 BC, and Jerusalem was destroyed in 586. Captivity and division followed. When God somehow transported Ezekiel to this valley, all he could see were dried-up, bleached-out, and separated bones. Not skeletons of people, but bones; very many and very dry (v. 2).

At this point, God asked Ezekiel a question, "Son of man, can these bones live?" God didn't ask this question because He didn't know the answer; He asked it because Ezekiel didn't know. (The prophet was probably like, "You're asking me?")

If the people of God and the nation of Israel are going to be "reborn" (chapter 37), how is it going to happen, and what will it look like? When it does come about, what will be the result? That is what chapter 37 describes.

Ezekiel's Proclamation (1–10)

The prophet sounds like an evangelical pastor, for his sermon has three points. He speaks about bones. In fact, these bones of verse 1 are just like the bones of the Negro spiritual. As far as the prophet could see, there were very many bones, and they were very dry. These bones describe the chosen people: dead, dry, desperate; it's not a pretty picture.

God asked the prophet, "Can these bones live?" What was going to make a difference in an otherwise hopeless situation? The Word of God (v. 4) and the Spirit of God (v. 9). Ezekiel was to share God's Word, and he was to call on God's Spirit. The word *breath* is the word for wind or spirit. When God blows on things, it comes to life. God blew on Adam at Creation (Genesis 2:7), He blew on His Word (2 Timothy 3:16–17), He blew on His disciples for empowerment (John 20:22), and one day, He will blow on Israel and His chosen people.

He spoke of bodies. As he preached, in the vision, the bones began to rattle and move and come together. Tendons and muscle and flesh were added, but it was just a completed corpse; no breath, no life. Very much like the land today.

He spoke of breath. Finally, breath came into them, and they came to life and stood up like a mighty army. I'm sure as the preacher finishes his sermon, he wonders what is this all about. (You've probably never said that after your pastor's sermon.)

God's Interpretation (11–14)

The really awesome thing about Zeke's sermon is that you don't have to wonder what it means. God Himself is about to give the interpretation. Since 1948, many Jewish people have left their current homes and moved back to Israel. The bones that have been scattered and lifeless for hundreds of years are coming together.

Mostly, this passage is yet before us. One day, perhaps soon, God is going to come and begin bringing His people out of the grave and to their land; the bones will be coming together and coming home, but not just to their land. They will come to their Lord (v. 14).

Israel's Glorification (15–28)

A divided kingdom was never God's ideal, but He will bring His people back together. The two kingdoms (Northern and Southern), seen as two sticks, will be brought together as one. God is determined and responsible for Israel being revived, revitalized, restored, and reestablished.

God then unfolds a series of promises, thirteen in all, that will be a result of this great restoration. Look at this list:

1. God will personally find Israel and gather the people from out of the nations (v. 21a).
2. God will bring them again into their land, which will be restored to them (v. 21b).
3. God will make one nation of the two (v. 22a).

4. God will set one King over the nations (v. 22b, 24a).
5. God will ensure the unity of the restored Kingdom, which will never again be divided (v. 22c).
6. God will be their Lord and will ensure that they never again serve idols (v. 23a).
7. God will save them, cleanse them, and establish an intimate personal relationship with them (v. 23b).
8. God will enable them to walk in obedience to His law (v. 24b).
9. God will establish them in their land forever (v. 25).
10. God will establish His new covenant of peace with them (v. 26a).
11. God will multiply them in their land, and they will enjoy His favor and peace (v. 26b).
12. God will establish His sanctuary among them and personally dwell there forever (v. 26c, 27).
13. God will make Israel an example and a testimony to the nations of the world of His saving grace (v. 28).

If you want to know what all of this will look like and how it will develop, go back and read Ezekiel 36:22–26.

In summary, this amazing vision of a valley of dry bones tells me that God is not finished with Israel. So remember this:

- When the nations of the world place Israel in the crosshairs, just know, God is not finished with Israel.
- When the Hitlers, Husseins, Ayatollahs, and Soleimanis predict her doom, just know, God is not finished with Israel.
- When all the news reports seem nasty, negative, hateful, and hostile, just know, God is not finished with Israel.
- When the tanks are rolling in, armies are gathering, and missiles are discharged, just know, God is not finished with Israel.

- When Islam constructs a mosque on the ancient Temple Mount and seeks to deny Jews and Christians access to this sacred site, just know, God is not finished with Israel.
- When her Messiah was denied, rejected, crucified, and buried in a borrowed tomb, just know, God is not finished with Israel.

"I will be their God, and they will be My people. And the nations will know that I am the Lord who sanctifies Israel" (Ezekiel 37:27b–28a).

1. When you hear the "valley of dry bones," what comes to your mind?
2. Why does God so love and desire Israel?
3. What should be our response to our Israeli friends? How should we pray for them?
4. Read again the thirteen promises made by God to Israel. What do these mean?
5. God is not finished with Israel. What are some ways you can pray for or be involved in a mission or ministry there?

Valley of Jezreel (Decision)

Joel 3

Joel is called a minor prophet, but the book of Joel contains a major message. In fact, as I read it again today, it was like opening up this morning's *USA Today* newspaper. As I write (April 2020), our nation is struggling greatly from a virus called COVID-19. To date, millions of people are being impacted, infected, and quarantined. We learned yesterday that hundreds of thousands of Americans have died. In addition to the death rate, many other things are creating a national disaster. Businesses are closed, schools are closed, churches cannot meet, and the economy is on a daily rollercoaster ride of uncertainty. Honestly, it's crazy and a little scary.

This is not the first time our nation has faced a crisis, and it won't be the last. In fact, there have been plagues, epidemics, pandemics, floods, wars, stock market crashes, fires, 9-11, and on and on. As Christians, we have to understand that God not only allows these events, in many ways He sends them to accomplish His purposes. And He will again.

The prophet Joel faced a similar scenario and wrote about it. There had been a serious plague of locusts and drought (chapter 1). There was an invasion coming (chapter 2). And there would one day be a "war to end all wars" in the land of Israel. And once it's over, the Lord Jesus will reign from His throne in Jerusalem (chapter 3).

God didn't have to send the armies of the world to Judah to get his people's attention and drive them to their knees; all he needed was a swarm of bugs. That did the job. At times, God uses natural disasters, terrorist attacks, economic collapse, bacteria, and viruses to not only get our attention but to accomplish His sovereign purpose.

The book of Joel is a small but amazing book. It starts with locusts but ends with the Lord. It begins with tragedy but concludes with triumph. Chapters 1 and 2 are about judgment, but chapter 3 is about Jesus. God has an answer for all three events. After the current events of chapter 1 and the locusts and drought, God said, "You better get right" (1:14). As the prophet warns his readers in chapter 2 of coming events, the invasion of an army and destruction, God tells them to "get ready" (2:12–17). Lastly, there are Christocentric events in chapter 3: The Lord will return, Armageddon will happen, the millennial will be ushered in, and God tells them to "be ready" (3:9–17).

Here, we are focused on the future events of chapter 3 when the Lord, having decided to return and act, will bring about His plan, His judgment, His conquest, and His reign. And can I remind you, "His plans cannot be thwarted" (Job 42:2).

The Likely Place This Is

Only the prophet Joel uses the term "valley of Jehoshaphat" (v. 2, 12). Some writers believe this to be between Jerusalem and the Mount of Olives, also called the Kidron. Though this is a strategic location, it is certainly not large enough to host such an event.

A better idea is in the place called Mount Megiddo, overlooking the Jezreel Valley (Revelation 16:16). The word *Armageddon* is made up of two words: Har (mountain) and Megiddo (to strike, kill, or massacre). Megiddo is the mountain of desolation.

When we visit Megiddo, located on the southwest end of the Carmel Mountain range, it is very easy to see many of the twenty-three civilizations on this mound. Mount Megiddo borders the Jezreel Valley, which is over 350 square miles in size, much larger than the Kidron. This location is also important historically; it was a crossroads, of sorts. Two major trade routes intersected at this location: the King's Highway and the Via Maris (or the Way of the Sea). Interestingly, when Commander Napoleon Bonaparte stood on Megiddo in 1799, he called this valley "a natural battlefield."

Indeed, it has been. This is where Deborah and Barak defeated the Canaanites (Judges 4–5), Gideon slew the Midianites (Judges 7), Ahaziah killed Jehu (2 Kings 9), and Josiah was slain by Pharaoh Neco of Egypt (2 Kings 23). Each of these uprisings will pale in comparison to the one yet to come. For God will draw all the nations of the world to this place for the Battle of Armageddon (Revelation 16).

Joel records some of the reasons for the necessity of this battle. Beyond the obvious of their rejection of Messiah, the prophet points out how the world has treated God's chosen people. Look at the phrases he records: "scattered among the nations," "divided up my land," "treated them like slaves," "cast lots and traded," "robbed my treasury," and they trivialized holy things: "my precious treasure in your temples."

My friends, our God is gracious, merciful, loving, forgiving, and patient. But once He has decided (v. 14), He is going to act. Joel pictures the nations being harvested like grapes or grain "put in the sickle" (v. 13). The "winepress is full, and the vats are overflowing" (v. 13b), and now the grapes are trampled underfoot, and all the juice is squeezed out to make wine. On this day, it will be blood, not juice, that is flowing. The Lord will utterly crush the nations of this world. What is left is destruction and carnage like we have never known. Revelation 14:20 says the blood will be so deep and wide, it will come up to a horse's bridle (about five feet high) and go out some two hundred miles. Whether this language is literal or symbolic, you get the picture.

The Love God Has

In spite of how the Hebrews reacted toward Jesus and responded to Him—they rejected Him and crucified Him—God still refers to them as "My people" and this area as "My land." "They are My inheritance, and this is My silver and gold/temple things" (vv. 2, 3, 5). God has not torn up His covenant, abandoned His people, or forgotten His great love, and one day, He will gather this preserved remnant, come to their aid, and utterly defeat their enemies. He is a God of mercy and grace.

And He will do the same for all who know Him. He will never leave you, abandon you, forget you, or break His covenant with you. Why? You've been grafted in, and our Lord is a God of mercy and grace. Can I get an amen?

The Lord Is Coming Again

As you scan the verses of Joel's sermon, seventy-three in total, you notice the prophet looking; he looks back (chapter 1), ahead (chapter 2), and forward (chapter 3). Let's do that too. Let's jump forward to that time when the Lord appears, defeats His enemies, rights all the wrongs, and occupies His rightful throne.

A.   The Lord Returns (16–17)

As the nations of the world begin to gather in the Jezreel Valley, all of a sudden, the Lord will appear, and His glory will illumine the universe (Matthew 24:30). Christ will be seated on His majestic white stallion, and on His head will be a crown (Revelation 19:11–12, 16). His eyes will be like flames of fire, and His garment will be dipped in blood (Revelation 19:12–13). With Him will be His righteous army: saints from throughout the ages and the awesome angelic host of heaven (Revelation 19:14).

Have you ever been on the front row of a concert, play, or sporting event? There are no distractions or hindrances; all is in full view. Child of God, when He returns, you'll be with Him to see it all unfold – front row!

B.   The Lord Restores (18–21)

"And in that day" (v. 18), things are going to be different. Today, Jewish people have no temple on the Temple Mount of Jerusalem; instead, a Muslim mosque is there. However, God promises to restore His city and dwell in Zion. Jerusalem, He said, "will be holy." His land will also be "transformed." All of the waste places of the land will become like Eden, and her desert like the garden of the Lord (Isaiah

51:3). In chapter 1, there was no food and no harvest. The land flowing with milk and honey will also have water and wine.

Jerusalem is the only ancient city that wasn't built on or near a water source; Nineveh was, Rome was, Babylon was, and all the cities of Egypt were near the Nile. Jerusalem was not. But, during Jesus's Millennial Reign, a river will flow from the temple, half toward the Mediterranean and half down to the Dead Sea (Zechariah 14:8). The prophet Ezekiel seems to describe this river (chapter 47).

C. The Lord Reigns (21)

The prophets saw the glory of God leave the temple years before, and the temple was destroyed. Now, a new temple is built, and God's glorious Son is not only present; He is on the throne. This city now has a new name: *Jehovah Shammah,* the Lord is present (Ezekiel 48:30–35).

World conditions seem to give a strong indication that time is short, and God's prophetic clock is about to chime the midnight hour. Are you prepared for His arrival?

"Thy Kingdom come" (Matthew 6:10).

"Even so, come, Lord Jesus" (Revelation 22:20).

Exploration Guide

1. What is the difference between a major and minor prophet?
2. Have you ever lived through a plague or pandemic? What did this mean to your daily routine? Economy? Health?
3. What is the meaning of "millennial," and what are the three major millennial views?
4. Why is Megiddo/Jezreel an ideal battle site?
5. What are some of the things God will restore after He comes?

Valley of Jordan River

Matthew 3

My home in Alabama faces the beautiful Tennessee River. Every day in the Tennessee River Valley, we get to watch deer, skunks, fox, and eagles. (Yes, I know it's tough, but someone has to do it.)

There is a similar place to this in the Holy Land. It's the Jordan River Valley, which is the border between Israel and Jordan. The Jordan River runs from the Golan Heights to the Dead Sea; it is primarily the area around Jericho, north of the sea that is associated with this name.

Biblically and historically, this area is very significant. It is where Joshua led the Israelites into the Promised Land. It was also from this location that the prophet Elijah was taken to heaven in a fiery chariot. In this area, John the Baptist preached, ministered, and baptized; one day, his cousin Jesus came down from Galilee and wanted to be baptized. So in this area, Israel went through, Jesus went down, and Elijah went away. Today, this area is called Qasr al-Yahud.

There are two areas used by tourists as baptismal sites in Israel. Yardenit is in Galilee, just south of the Sea of Galilee. It is green, lush, and festive. There you'll find hundreds of pilgrims, a nice gift shop, and a festive atmosphere. Though this is the Jordan River, it's not where Jesus was immersed by John. Qasr al-Yahud is the more authentic location. Why? It was where John was located, Jesus came from Galilee, and it was near the place of temptation.

Today, Qasr al-Yahud is in what is called "the land of the monasteries." There are several unfinished and abandoned churches and monasteries left from the time of the Six-Day War. This area is lined with barbed wire fences, it's dotted with warning signs, and it's booby-trapped with mines. Still, some eight hundred thousand visitors come to these waters annually. Many believe this is the third most prominent spot in Jesus's life, after Bethlehem (Church of the Nativity) and Jerusalem (Church of the Holy Sepulcher). It's a worthwhile place because Jesus came to be baptized here.

Baptism is a biblical word and it has its roots in theology. Christian baptism is the full immersion of a believer in water. This is seen as an act of obedience to our Lord's command. It identifies the recipient with the death, burial, and resurrection of Christ. Believers are baptized in the name of (authority) the Father, the Son, and the Holy Spirit. As one is raised from the water, it likens them to Christ's resurrection and their walking in a new life. In Baptist church life, baptism is seen as one of two church ordinances (the other being the Lord's Supper), and as such, it is a prerequisite to the privileges of church membership.

Every pastor can tell you stories of baptismal experiences. I have some that I guarantee are true, but if I told you the names and church, I'd have to enter the witness protection program! I may put them in a book one day, when I'm closer to retirement. For now, just let your mind wonder.

I am reminded of a trip to Qasr al-Yahud last summer with a group from Alabama. Another pastor was with me, and I asked him to oversee the baptisms. As he was concluding, a white dove descended and perched on the handrail going into the water. No, we didn't see the heavens open or hear the voice of God, but it was a moment none in our group will forget. If you've read Matthew 3:13–17, you'll understand why.

Jesus came to the river to be baptized, but not as a means of salvation or to wash away His sin; He came to inaugurate His earthly work, paint for us a picture, and provide an example. Sadly, many have a warped idea about this practice today. Some view it as a means of obtaining grace and thus being regenerated. Wrong. Others believe it's a practice for infants or babies that will guarantee their one-day salvation. No. Still some see it as nothing more than a modern fad (and a way to get a new T-shirt). Incorrect.

There are three types of baptism spoken of in scripture: spiritual (1 Corinthians 12:13), water (Matthew 3:16, Acts 8:39), and suffering (or fire) (Matthew 3:11, Mark 10:38–39). We are talking here about water baptism, which is totally immersing true believers in a tub or pool of water, or a river, and raising them back up. (Please don't leave them under; it will ruin the meaning and put a damper on your service.)

It's not my intention here to discuss who is to be baptized. I hope you understand it's for believers in Jesus who have repented of their sins and who have become recipients of His grace through faith in Christ's finished work. Nor is my intent to debate the method, or how. The word means to immerse, plunge, or dip into water; case closed. Finally, it's not about when. Baptism is for believers in Christ who are old enough to understand what this means. This disqualifies infants or babies (and some older nonbelievers).

My desire is for us to answer why? Why should a person be baptized in water? In answering this, we will develop why this practice is important to the Lord's work and His church. Maybe we'll also squelch some other fallacies.

To Follow Christ's Example (Matthew 3:13–17)

Remember, Jesus wasn't being baptized in order to be saved or have His sins washed away; He didn't want to get a cool T-shirt. He was providing an example for us to follow, and if He thought it was critical enough to walk many miles from Nazareth to this location, it must have been an important matter. Very soon after the conversions of Paul, Cornelius, and Lydia, they all were baptized.

As an Act of Obedience (Matthew 28:19–20)

Jesus's final words to the disciples were to take the Gospel to lost humanity: "Go, therefore and make disciples of all the nations, baptizing them." After we make disciples, and as we mature them, we are to mark them, in baptism. If you have genuinely been saved and have the opportunity to do so, choosing not to be baptized is an act of rebellion and disobedience.

As a Public Expression of Faith (Romans 10:9–10, Colossians 2:12)

Though one's faith and salvation are very personal, it was never intended to be private. We are to abide in Christ, announce to the world, and affiliate with a local church. When we are baptized, we do each of these things. I've often said that as someone is baptized, their life is preaching a sermon on the death and resurrection of Jesus.

It Identifies You with Christ's Death and Resurrection (Romans 6:1–11)

Paul's letter to believers in Rome is saturated with deep and rich truth (as is all the Word). Romans 6 is one of the key chapters in all the Bible. Chapter 6 reminds us we were dead in sin, Jesus died for sin, so now we can be dead to sin. People, as they say, that will preach. Listen to what he writes in these few verses: We who died to sin (v. 2), we too might walk in newness of life (v. 4), united with Him in His resurrection (v. 5), our old self was crucified (v. 6a), we are no longer slaves to sin (v. 6b), freed from sin (v. 7), we shall live with Him (v. 8), we are dead to sin but alive to Christ Jesus (v. 11). Honestly, we should all camp out in the book of Romans for a while.

It Connects You to the Local Church (Acts 2:41–47)

Baptism today is viewed as a local church ordinance (a prescribed religious rite) that is intended to demonstrate the adherent's faith. As such, this act should be administered by your local church leaders or their designees. When we are baptized, we are saying, "I understand the terms of what it means to be a member of this church, and I submit to her leaders and guidelines, and I will support her mission and testimony by living an exemplary life."

Sadly, in my denomination, the number of baptisms has been on a steady decline for the last thirty years. We need to get back to the basics of preaching, missions, and evangelism so we can stir the waters of our baptistries.

But when we resort to baptism becoming a fad, a group activity, or a public spectacle, I'm afraid we've missed the point. I hope your baptism was about more than just getting a T-shirt.

Exploration Guide

N
W ← → E
S

1. What do you recall about your baptism?
2. What does baptism mean? Is it necessary for one's salvation? Is the method important?
3. When should a person be baptized?
4. How is being baptized similar to preaching a sermon?
5. What are the types of baptism spoken of in scripture?
6. If you are a follower of Jesus and you've not yet been biblically baptized, why not consider doing that now? (Your pastor will gladly discuss this with you.)

Mount Precipice

Luke 4

Mount Precipice is a name given to a hill located on the southern edge of Nazareth, Jesus's childhood home. Though the word *precipice* doesn't appear in the biblical text, what it describes certainly does.

A precipice is a very steep rock face or cliff; it's normally very tall. The one read about in Luke's Gospel is almost thirteen hundred feet high. It's not just high; it's also large. To illustrate just how large this peak is, in 2009, Pope Benedict XVI celebrated a Mass on this site, and over forty thousand people attended. (By way of contrast, when Jesus lived in Nazareth, the population of the city was about four hundred.)

In recent years, this mountain has been used as a quarry, but it is now abandoned. A highway runs through this mountain, and it connects Afula and the Jezreel Valley to Nazareth. Archaeological excavations have found caves in the sides of this mountain with human remains that are very old. Some believe these were burial spots of victims or criminals who were thrown off the cliff. For our purposes, that is conjecture at best, but we do believe the account recorded in Luke's Gospel.

I've been to Nazareth and on top of Mount Precipice many times. In fact, it's an area I look for as I drive from Tel Aviv or Jerusalem to Nazareth. I now know how to recognize this cliff and Mount Tabor off to the right. When I spot those sites, I can get my bearings straight and know we're almost to Nazareth. This amazing city has become like a second home so it's always good to get to Nazareth.

Nazareth, today, is a busy city of about eighty-five thousand residents. It has been called the Arab Capital of Israel, and it is a melting pot of many peoples, religions, and businesses. In Jesus's day, it was much smaller; the people were shepherds, stone masons, weavers, and farmers. This is where Jesus was brought back to and where He grew "in wisdom and stature and in favor with God and man" (Luke 2:52). However, it was much different when He came back there as an adult.

Get this picture: At about age thirty, Jesus leaves Nazareth and travels to the Jordan River Valley; His cousin John is preaching and baptizing, and Jesus is baptized by him. After His baptism, Jesus is led by the Spirit into the wilderness to be tempted by the devil. After forty days and nights of temptation (and prayer), Jesus begins to preach, minister, and call disciples. So excited about all that's happening, He goes back to His hometown and takes His ministry there.

This is where our text is, and this was where some of His irritation with the religious crowd began. (I'm sure he still gets irritated with them.) You could make these comparisons: In Galilee, Jesus was praised, but in Nazareth, he was persecuted. In Galilee, the people sought to know him; in Nazareth, they sought to kill him. In Galilee, Jesus was there to build the people up; in Nazareth, the people were there to throw Jesus down. Amazing, huh? In his hometown, nonetheless.

From our passage, we learn the following:

The Closest May Be the Hardest (24)

In ministry, it often seems that those closest to us are the hardest to reach. For whatever reason, this is no doubt true. It was even true for God's Son; while many other places welcomed Him and followed Him, his hometown did not. "A prophet is not welcomed in His hometown" (24).

That's kind of frightening. I recently moved back to my hometown, and my office is in my home church; pray for me, would you?

People's Opinions of You Can Turn on a Dime (22, 28)

Look at these two verses and ask yourself, How can this be? In a matter of six verses, the accolades have stopped, the criticism has begun, and Jesus is about to be run out of town. I think of this story every time I preach in Nazareth, and I have two goals: preach the Word faithfully and don't get run out of town.

At Times, the Truth Can Lead You into Trouble (25–29)

Jesus is truth incarnate, and He speaks the truth. As He addresses this "Jewish gathering," He uses some gentile illustrations; the Hebrews of history had rejected God and believed not, but a gentile widow and leper believed. The implication to this crowd is, you're just like your ancestors, you refuse to believe, and they didn't like it. Was it a truthful statement? Yes. Did they accept it? No.

So what did they do? Their goal was to run Jesus out of town and throw him off Mount Precipice to his death. This is partly what is meant by the idea of stoning someone. Stoning was a means of punishment resulting in death. This didn't mean just throwing rocks at them. Often, this form of punishment meant throwing the victim off of a high mountain or cliff. If the fall didn't kill them, then they would throw boulders down or hurl rocks at the person to finish the job. No doubt, their goal was Jesus's death.

The Father Protected and Preserved His Life, and He Will Yours (30)

Let me make a big and bold statement to you: "You are immortal until God is finished with you." The enemy and your enemies are not greater than God, and His plans cannot and will not be thwarted. Go ahead and shout, "Glory," and stop living in fear; move forward in faith.

The Leading Deterrent Most of Us Encounter Is Not Our Location; It's the Unbelief of Others (Mark 6:5–6)

In Mark's account of this story, he doesn't point out Jesus's near-death experience but rather the locals' unbelief. It was hard for Jesus to do His real ministry there because of their unbelief. A lack of faith produces a lack of results. Jesus could do no mighty work there. Why? They didn't believe, and they had no faith. Familiar people? Yes. Religious people? Yes. Sincere people? Yes. But they lacked faith, and Jesus "marveled" at this. If your life or ministry or church is not experiencing the mighty touch of God, it may be time to take a look at your faith.

Speaking of Nazareth

I often think of Nathanael's question to Philip in John 1:46: "Can any good thing come out of Nazareth?" Philip responds, "Come and see." Today, something good is still coming out of Nazareth. Did you know that the largest evangelical school in all of Israel is in Nazareth? For almost a hundred years, the Nazareth Baptist School (NBS) has been "building the rising generations, glorifying Jesus Christ through distinctive education." This school of over one thousand students has been impacting the community, the culture, and the country for many years. The Nazareth Baptist School is peerless and stands alone among the forty-eight Christian schools in Israel. NBS is the only K-12 Christian school in Israel that

- is Baptist as well as evangelical,
- is recognized by the Israeli Ministry of Education,
- mandates Bible class and age-graded chapel attendance,
- sponsors evangelistic programs, such as summer programs, sports, music, and arts,
- has a biblically based leadership development program for its staff,

- is a partner with Dr. Jay Strack's Student Leadership University, and
- offers cross-cultural school partnerships and university experience.

If you would like more information about the Nazareth Baptist School, contact Friends of Nazareth in Florence, Alabama, visit the website friendsofnazareth.org, or email me at roger@ friendsofnazareth.org.

"Come and see" (John 1:46b).

Exploration Guide

1. What do you most love about your hometown? What do you hate about it (if anything)?
2. Why is it that those closest to us may be the hardest to reach?
3. When has speaking the truth about a matter gotten you into trouble?
4. When you read the statement, "You are immortal until God is finished with you," how did you feel about that? Do you agree or disagree? Why?
5. Why could Jesus do no mighty work in Nazareth? How may that challenge you?

Mount of Beatitudes

Matthew 5–7

One of the great joys of ministry is that I've had the honor of meeting some great preachers and hearing some terrific sermons. I recall one day asking Michelle, "How many really great preachers are there?" She replied, "I'm not sure of the number, but probably one less than you're thinking." (We are still married, and I do still love her.)

Think of these great preachers: W. A. Criswell, Adrian Rogers, Jonathan Edwards, R. G. Lee, J. Harold Smith, C. H. Spurgeon, Billy Graham, Jerry Vines, and Billy Sunday. Wow, what a list (and there are so many more). I also think of some well-known sermons that I've either heard or read or just know about: "The Infallible Word of God" (Criswell), "Our Ascended Lord" (Vines), "Sinners in the Hands of an Angry God" (Edwards), "Payday Someday" (Lee), "God's Three Deadlines" (Smith), "Who Is Jesus?" (Graham), and "Heaven and Hell" (Spurgeon). Honestly, our work and calling are not about great preachers or sermons; it's about a great God and a great story we are blessed to tell.

But no doubt the greatest Preacher Who ever lived (and still lives) is Jesus, and He has certainly preached the greatest sermon. We call it the Sermon on the Mount. There are 111 verses of this sermon. It doesn't have three alliterated points, a funny opening story, or a cute concluding poem. There is a great introduction that gets your attention and multiple illustrations that get His point across. In the end, the listeners are presented with two options: hear his sermon and act on its contents, or hear it and don't. One response is wise, and the other is foolish. Evidently, the crowd was attentive, and they were amazed at His teaching.

Some say there are dozens of approaches to understanding and interpreting this sermon; clearly, that was not our Lord's desire. Some view this sermon as God's plan for our salvation. If you ever hope to get to heaven, you must obey these rules and live by them, perfectly. No, that can't be right. Others say this treatise is a charter for world peace, which would be the outcome if all nations merely adopted it. That too has been rejected.

A third idea is that this sermon is not for today, but it describes what life will be like during the Millennial Reign of Christ. Though these ideas will be present then and will be seen during His Kingdom, surely this teaching is more a result of faith in the present and not a future-tense idea.

The key is found in 5:20: "For I say unto you that unless your righteousness surpasses that of the scribes and Pharisees, you will not enter the kingdom of Heaven." Confronting the man made artificial righteousness that the law produces, a new Master came forth with a new message, a true and vital righteousness that begins in the heart. That is, when our hearts are made right by grace and through faith, our lives will begin to live right and look right. No doubt this is the idea.

In this book, you'll also learn about Mount Eremos, where Jesus delivered this masterpiece. Mount Eremos is located on the Sea of Galilee, just above Capernaum. Some refer to this as the Mount of Beatitudes, because of His statements in the opening verses (vv. 3–12).

As we begin to scale this sermonic mountain, there are scores of illustrations and applications we could make to our spiritual lives. Space will not permit us to detail all of these, but let me suggest a few characteristics of the Kingdom Saint:

They Learn How to Deal with Unfair People (5:11–12)

Here is a fact: Life is not fair, and people can, and will, be difficult at times. They will talk bad to you and about you. This might be your boss, coworker, neighbor, coach, or friend. When this happens, it is easy to get defensive and start to react. Jesus said when this happens to us, we are blessed and we should rejoice; talk about a relational paradigm shift. No doubt His crowd was taken back by the new blessing.

They Make a Difference Where They Are (5:13–16)

We live in a world that is bland and distasteful; it is bleak and dark, so Jesus tells His followers to be salt and to be light. Both of these items make a difference when let out. Don't stay in the saltshaker, and do get out from under the basket; you can make a difference for Christ's Kingdom. Let your light shine today.

They Will Learn to Resolve Conflict (5:21–24, 38–44)

Our world does well at making foes, but Jesus tells us to "make friends ... quickly" (5:25). Do you harbor resentment, hold grudges, or have enemies? Jesus reminds us that this type of attitude not only affects our daily walk; it will ruin our worship. This radical concept needs to be heralded and taught today as much as ever. The hatred and hostility among families, political parties, and theological groups is at an all-time high. Evidently, we aren't practicing Jesus's words; He said to love and forgive and pray. I'm with Him.

They Will Be True to Their Word (5:33–37)

Often, we think of the sins of the tongue merely as things like lying, gossiping, slandering, cursing, and the like. Jesus warns us about making vows we cannot keep. Believers are to be people of truth in what they say and how they live. It's as simple as this: let your yes be yes and your no be no; anything else is often evil intent.

They Desire to Be Righteous, Not Self-Righteous (6:2–18)

Why do we as believers do what we do? Is it with a heart desiring to please God or to be noticed by others? Jesus uses three examples: giving, praying, and fasting. Interesting thought: The text says *when* you give, *when* you pray, and *when* you fast. It doesn't say *if* you do. The clear teaching and assumption of Jesus is that His followers would do these things, not to gain His favor but because they've been made new in His image.

They Will Be Otherworldly, Not Worldly (6:19–24)

If all we do in life is for here and not there, we miss God's intention. It's often said, "You can't take it with you, but you can send it on ahead." Jesus warns us of rust and robbers, moths and men who only desire to hurt and steal. I often think of all the wealth that was lost aboard the *Titanic*. Friends, we cannot serve God and money; our "wealth" is a great blessing, but it's a terrible master.

They Will Trust the Lord to Meet Their Needs (6:25–34)

At least four times in these verses, Jesus speaks of an anxious heart dealing with "worry." To help us grasp this lesson, He mentions our food and our fashion, what we eat and what we wear. In the same way God feeds the birds and clothes the fields, He will take care of your needs. So don't worry. Rather, we are to seek God and live in a godly way. As I live this way, it is God's responsibility and desire to take care of His own.

They Will Look to Their Own Life, Not Others (7:1–5)

I always say, one of the few verses unbelievers can quote is verse 1: "Judge not lest you be judged." So true. Each of us need to worry about our own self and our life. I need to deal with the large logs in my eye and not worry about the dainty dust in yours. You need to do the same. If we refuse to do so, Jesus said, we are hypocrites who are merely playing a game.

They Will Be Faithful and Fruitful (7:13–23)

Jesus spoke of two roads and two trees. Are you traveling the narrow path? Are you producing the proper fruit? Don't believe everything you hear or see; the true and faithful ones are "doing the will of the Father who is in heaven" (v. 21).

Following this incredible sermon, the Lord says, "Therefore" (v. 24). I once explained to my congregation, "When you read 'therefore,' you need to ask, what is it there for?"

We are to take all the items Jesus spoke of and act on them. When we do so, we are wise. You may not be building a home, but you are building a marriage, family, career, or life. The Kingdom Saint will desire to know God's will and apply His Word. To refuse this sermon and to not apply these truths is like the foolish man who built his house on the sand. Surely you know the outcome.

So friends, what will it be? Will you hear and obey? Will you respond, or will you rebel? Will you be wise, or will you be foolish? Kingdom Saints respond in Kingdom ways.

Exploration Guide

1. What's your favorite sermon? Who are some of your favorite preachers?
2. What is the purpose for this particular sermon?
3. What does the biblical idea of righteousness mean?

4. This sermon says "when" you pray, give, and fast, not "if." How are these disciplines true in your life? Your church?

5. What were Jesus's instructions about resolving conflict? Is there a matter you need to deal with or resolve?

6. Based on this sermon, are you being wise or foolish?

Mount Eremos

Mark 1, Matthew 28

One of the most fascinating places I like to visit when in the Holy Land goes by a name you've probably never heard (unless you speak Greek). Jesus would often go to a secluded and private place (Mark 1:35), and the term used to describe it is *Eremos Topos*. These Greek words depict a solitary or lonely place. Such a place is described by each of the Gospel writers.

This type of place would have been on a steep hillside or a rocky location. If it were good soil, it would have been planted by a farmer. If you were looking for a place to meet or hang out with your friends, you wouldn't choose farm areas, for you might damage the crops. So you would seek out a place that was remote, barren, or not cultivated. There are not many places like that around Tiberias, and only a few spots would qualify as an eremos topos.

One such place is located just above the road between Tabgtha and Capernaum. This is the site where many scholars believe Jesus used to pray, meet, and train. A Christian pilgrim named Egeria in the fourth century wrote of a long-held tradition that there is a cave in the hillside at the Seven Springs (Tabgtha), where our Lord gathered. This place is called Mount Eremos. The view from this spot offers a magnificent picture of the entire lake and surrounding villages.

For Jesus and His followers, it would have become a very special and incredibly spiritual location. What type of place was this?

A Place of Meeting

Jesus had at least two places where he would meet His disciples or find solitude from the growing crowds and His busy schedule. One of these places was in Jerusalem and one in Galilee. Interestingly, there was a cave in both spots, which would have been dry havens during the rainy season.

In Jerusalem, this place was in the Garden of Gethsemane. John 18:1–2 describes this place and relates how often Jesus went there: "When Jesus had spoken these words, He went forth with His disciples over the ravine of the Kidron where there was a garden in which He entered with His disciples. Now Judas also, who was betraying Him, knew the place. For Jesus had often met there with His disciples." It makes much sense. This location was close to the city, to water, to food, and it provided shade and shelter; a perfect meeting place.

In Galilee, well, that's different. Galilee describes a very large area. The northern part of the whole country can be called Galilee. This area would include areas from the Great Sea to the Jordan River Valley, Nazareth, Caesarea, Cana, Nain, the Jezreel Valley, and all the area around the Sea of Galilee. So when Jesus said, "I'll meet you on the mountain in Galilee," which one did He mean? His disciples would have known; it was Mount Eremos (Matthew 8:1, 14:22–27, 28:16; Mark 1:35, 3:13, 6:46).

We men totally understand that. At every age and stage of life, we have a location we know of to meet with other men. It might be the gym, a coffee shop, a local restaurant, or the barber shop. Men need a place to meet. Eremos was their man cave.

A Place of Mingling

This was not just the designated spot to meet; it was also where Jesus and His disciples would hang out, laugh, learn, and chat. Jesus had followers from different areas, families, and backgrounds. They would need to come together as a team if they were to conquer the world.

Can you imagine overhearing some of the stories they recounted or questions they asked?

"I didn't know what she was trying to do when she reached in to touch his garment."

"Did you see their faces when the ceiling began to crumble around them, and they lowered that lame man down?"

"Jesus, how did you come to choose each of us?"

"Are you ever going to tell us how you did that?"

"It was so cool when they began pouring out the water and it had become wine."

"Hey guys, wait; you forgot your basket."

I imagine these and many more stories were talked about and discussed. John's Gospel closes by saying, "There are also many other things which Jesus did, which if they were written in detail, I suppose that even the world itself would not contain the books that would be written" (John 21:25).

A Place of Mentoring

Jesus is teaching these guys how to live their lives, support His ministry, and do His work. There were no opportunities at a neighborhood seminary, and there was opposition at the synagogues. So Mount Eremos became a place to shape, mold, form, and mature an amazing but young band of followers.

A caution: These types of relationships can be the cause of great joy or profound sorrow. It had to break the heart of their mentor when Peter denied the Lord and when Judas betrayed Him. But here is a good motto: "It's never right to do the wrong thing, and it's never wrong to do the right thing." Mentoring and discipling young believers is always right, but at times, it may be messy.

A Place of Meditating

Jesus utilized this location to be with His disciples but also to be alone with His Father. Jesus needed time away from the crowds and activity, and He needed time alone to think over crucial matters and to pray about them. There were major decisions to make, needs to meet, lessons to teach, and a cross to bear. He would need this interaction with His Father.

It shouldn't even need to be said, but if the perfect Son of God needed that kind of place and those kinds of times, how much more do we?

A Place of Ministry

Mount Eremos is in a very strategic place on the shores of Galilee now, and it was just as strategic then. Major events like the delivering of the Sermon on the Mount (Matthew 5:7), the miraculous feeding of the five thousand (John 6), and the healing of the leper (Matthew 8) all happened within a stone's throw from this place. Capernaum, Jesus's Galilee home and headquarters, was a short distance away; as was Magdala, Tiberias, and some ancient roadways. Mount Eremos was like a hub of activity, with a spoke going up (Mount of Beatitudes), over (Tabgtha: loaves and fishes), and down (the leper colony at one of the Seven Springs).

A Place of Mission

After His resurrection, in one of His appearances, Jesus tells His disciples to meet Him in Galilee at the mountain. Which mountain, you may ask, or where in Galilee? They didn't have to ask. They knew which one without question. It was their place, very familiar, for they had met there many times before.

Once they arrived and had a time of worship (Matthew 28:17), Jesus then gave them a command which is still in effect today:

"All authority has been given to me in heaven and on earth. Go therefore and make disciples of all the nations, baptizing them in the name of the Father and the Son and the Holy Spirit, teaching them to observe all that I have commanded you; and lo, I am with you always, even to the ends of the age" (Matthew 28:18–20).

Sadly, most travelers to the Holy Land don't have a clue about Mount Eremos or this very special cave. I would guess that less than one-tenth of 1 percent of tourists in Galilee ever stop there or know about this place. People get out of the bus at Tabgtha and the Primacy of St. Peter and at Capernaum, but they miss a most special place right in between. Don't you dare make a similar mistake.

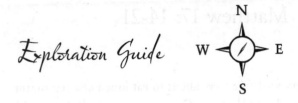

Exploration Guide

1. As a child, did you have a special place you liked to visit with close friends, or do you have one now?
2. Where were the two favorite places Jesus had to meet with His friends?
3. What might Jesus and the twelve discuss in their special place?
4. Do you have a solitary place where you can go to pray or meditate (Mark 1:35)? If not, you may want to designate a spot.
5. What is the Great Commission? What part are you and your church playing in fulfilling this mission?

Mount Herodium

Matthew 17: 14-21

I recall the day very well. We were about to eat lunch at a restaurant near Bethlehem I had never been to. Our group got off the bus, and I noticed that our guide had stopped and was pointing toward a hill a few miles away. (I'm sure I was like, "C'mon, Hani, let's eat; I'm starving," or, "What's the big deal? Another hill? Are you kidding me? They're everywhere, you know.")

All of a sudden, something he said resonated with me and our group. What mountain is this? Who had this built? Who was buried there? This is a man-made mountain? As in, you can move mountains. Hani had gotten my attention, and I wanted to learn more about a mountain called Herodium.

Honestly, I was not well schooled in the history of this site. Sure, I knew about Herod the Great and the other Herods, and I had preached many times about having a faith "that can move mountains," but I had yet to connect the many dots. I probably still can't do a thorough job, but for our purposes today, I want to point out a few things that may allow you to have a light-bulb moment, like I had that day outside Bethlehem.

Let's be honest; it's easy for even the schooled and scholarly to get confused or have a hard time distinguishing some Bible names. Herod is a perfect example. Is that a name or a title? Are we talking about Herod the Great or perhaps Agrippa, Antipas, or Archelaus? Did you say Herodians, Herodias, Herodian, or Herodium?

Herod was the name given to the leader and the family who ruled

Palestine immediately before Jesus's birth and during the first century. The history of this family was confusing and complex; in many ways, it was as dangerous as it was difficult. The most prominent of these Herods was the son of Antipater, who was of Idumaean descent, an Edomite, or a descendant of Esau. This son came to be known as Herod the Great.

This famed leader was not given this title because of his character or morality; really, he was more of a tyrant and a cruel leader. Herod the Great was narcissistic and jealous, and you better never challenge or oppose him. It was even said by Augustus that, "It is better to be Herod's hog than his son."

History tells us that Herod was appointed the procurator of Galilee when he was only twenty-five years of age. Mark Antony gave him a tetrarchy and later encouraged the Roman Senate to make him a king. Herod was technically a Jew; he observed many of the laws, customs, and dietary restrictions, but he was never accepted by the Jewish majority. He was appointed as king and coronated later by Caesar.

One can see why he may have been intimidated by a group of foreign Magi who arrived in Jerusalem, seeking the one "born King of the Jews" (Matthew 2:1–2). In fact, Matthew 2 is the only place in scripture where you read about this Herod (vv. 1–12, 16–19).

Extra-biblical literature and Jewish historians write about many of the accomplishments of Herod the Great. He was a visionary, a builder, and he provided for himself a luxurious lifestyle. Even today, one can view the remains of many of Herod's accomplishments; the Herodian stones of the Western Wall and the surrounding wall of Jerusalem, the Aqueduct that brought fresh water to Caesarea, Caesarea Maritima, Masada. Herod had many palaces and many projects.

Among those was the man-made mountain called Herodium.

Herod's Palace

Some have suggested Herod had eleven palaces, while others claim there were many more. It is said that each palace was built fairly close to the next, a one day's journey. So from the Northern Palace at Herodium to the Southernmost at Masada, all of these dwellings were a place of escape should things ever go wrong with either the Jews or with Caesar and the Romans. Many aspects of the back story of Herodium make it most interesting.

Where It Was Built

Herodium is not that far from Jerusalem and some of Herod's other famed buildings. So why just a few miles away? It is said that in 40 BC, the Parthian Empire conquered Judea, and in doing so, they named a new king. As Herod fled Jerusalem under the cover of night with some members of his family, his mother's chariot turned over, and she was trapped. Later, when she had miraculously escaped uninjured, Herod thanked the gods and declared he would one day be buried on the site. Thus, Herodium was built as a pleasure for his life and as a resting place in his death.

How It Was Built

Herodium is a self-made hill raised by scores of people over the years. Bucket by bucket, load by load, and one shovel after the other; dirt and rock and earth were literally moved. Today, we may use the term "raising a barn"; here, they were raising a mountain on which would be a palace that would one day be a tomb. One can only imagine the time and energy and resources needed to build your own mountain.

My Prayers

Just think about all the stories told about the people who built Herodium and how it was raised. The people of Jesus's day would have been well aware of this hill and how it came about. So when Jesus began to talk about their troubles being like a mountain that needed to be moved, they knew it was possible. In fact, with our faith and God's ability, it's not merely possible; it's probable.

It's worth noting that Jesus often used real-life situations like this to teach and illustrate. He did this when he talked about the lilies of the field (Matthew 6), the fields are white to harvest (John 4), the sower and the seed (Matthew 13), and a vineyard, wall, and tower (Mark 12). He did this again in Matthew 17. Let's look back over the situation that led to Jesus rebuking His disciples for their lack of faith and their inability to minister to a pressing need:

When they came to the crowd, a man came up to Jesus, falling on his knees before Him and saying, "Lord, have mercy on my son, for he is a lunatic and is very ill; for he often falls into the fire and often into the water. I brought him to Your disciples, and they could not cure him." And Jesus answered and said, "You unbelieving and perverted generation, how long shall I be with you? How long shall I put up with you? Bring him here to Me." And Jesus rebuked him, and the demon came out of him, and the boy was cured at once.

Then the disciples came to Jesus privately and said, "Why could we not drive it out?" And He said to them, "Because of the littleness of your faith; for truly I say to you, if you have faith the size of a mustard seed, you will say to this mountain, 'Move from here to there,' and it will move; and nothing will be impossible to you."

Here was a very crucial need: A man's son was possessed and needed to be delivered from the demon. Remember, Jesus came to "set the captives free" (Luke 4:18). So why couldn't His commissioned disciples perform this work? Jesus released the young man and rebuked the twelve.

Sometime later, the disciples are curious about why they couldn't perform this work. That's when Jesus references the moving of a mountain. The problem at hand was not the size of their need; it was the size of their faith.

In my office, I have a small bottle of mustard seeds I purchased at Nazareth Village. The bottle is the size of an old pill container, and there are about two hundred mustard seeds in it. The point I'm making is that they are small, really small, and compared to Herodium, well, there is no comparison. Jesus is reminding them, and us, that regardless of the size and scope of your personal mountain, it can be moved, for absolutely nothing will be impossible to you.

Let me ask you a question: What issues or concerns are you facing, and how are you approaching the solution? Are you relying on medication, counseling, or therapy? Please understand; I'm not opposed to any of these areas, for they certainly have their place. Others turn to alcohol, drugs, or some other so-called quick fix. Those things are never the answer. Jesus said the answer is faith, even if it is small.

I recall hearing a preacher say years ago, "A little bit of faith will bring a soul to heaven, but a whole lot of faith will bring heaven to a soul." I don't know how big your mountain is, but I do know we serve an awesome, powerful, and big God, and nothing is impossible with Him. Even moving mountains.

Exploration Guide

1. What are the names of some palaces you have visited? Where are they? What is their history?
2. What do you know about Herod the Great? (Consider searching his name and accomplishments.)
3. When you hear "moving mountains," what comes to your mind?
4. What are some other real-life stories or illustrations Jesus used to teach truth and apply?
5. What are the things in your life that need prayer and faith? Will you begin praying for these matters now, earnestly?

Mount Tabor (Transfiguration)

Luke 9

As I pen these words, our world is in chaos. COVID-19 is now a pandemic, and the reaction is unlike anything I have ever seen or experienced. Cancelations, closures, confusion, and a catastrophic stock market are all daily events. In the medical world, we talk of isolation, quarantine, swabs, masks, and even death. People, these are indeed strange times.

Speaking of the stock market, I recall saying to Michelle just a few weeks ago, "Babe, our retirement plan is rocking and rolling." Now, it's rolling … away. Let's hope it will soon be recovering. After several months of record-setting highs, we are now seeing some lows. It's up … and it's down. This not only describes the terrain of Israel; it reminds me of life.

It also reminds me of the setting surrounding today's reading: Luke 9:28–36. In the biblical text before and after the story of the Mount of Transfiguration, it's easy to notice the emotional valleys. In Luke 8, we read about a storm on the sea, demons, sickness, and even death. We learn of hard ministry situations and a lack of resources to feed a big crowd in chapter 9. All of these have a way of taking a toll on us. After the transfiguration, we notice another story of a demon-possessed boy, discouragement, and the death of a family member. Again, hard and emotional times: valleys.

Right in the midst of these taxing times is the amazing story of Jesus's transfiguration, that moment when His inner glory shone through His physical being, and He glowed with brightness. It was quite a moment. In fact, it was so awesome that Moses, Elijah, and God, His Father, all showed up. Don't you wish you could have been there? Hopefully, we would have done better than the inner circle of Peter, James, and John, who all fell asleep! This event has been called the Father's "seal of approval" after Peter's declaration, "You are the Christ ... the Son of God."

Two modern mountains are recognized as possible sites of this event. Mount Hermon is one, and Mount Tabor is the other. Mount Hermon is the northern boundary of Israel and is seen as a sacred mountain. Hermon is ninety-one hundred feet tall and is the highest mountain in Israel. Because it is high and in a close proximity to Caesarea Philippi, where Peter made his famed declaration (Matthew 16:18), many feel this is the logical spot.

Others hold to Mount Tabor being the likely location. *Tabor* means "height" and could be a play on words of a high mountain. Mount Tabor is located in Galilee, not far from Nazareth, Jesus's hometown. Many historians and church traditions hold to this being the actual location. There is a church/monastery atop Mount Tabor that is built over the presumed area.

The Mount of Transfiguration was a mountain of visions, visitors, and voices. It was a time for Peter's request, God's rebuke, and glory's return. Though this was a unique event, it reminds us that we can have a spiritual transformation daily as we surrender and obey. A pastor friend said of this story, "Jesus is in *prayer*, in *prophecy* (the law and the prophets), and in *preeminence*. He has no rival or equal."

The Transfiguration of Jesus

The word *transfigured* and the word *metamorphosis* mean "a change in appearance that comes from within." Jesus's glorified body illuminated His apparel in grand fashion. The Bright and Morning Star was now like the sun: dazzling in white. One of the many spiritual lessons from this encounter is that we can experience a daily transformation as we submit and surrender to our Lord. If we are to live the transformed life and experience His glory, there are a few things we must do.

We must *climb up*. To enjoy and experience the kind of spiritual life few know, we must be disciplined and determined. Whether it was Tabor or Hermon, to get to the top would have required some effort. Many Christians have a poor spiritual life because they aren't willing to grow and put forth the effort.

We need to *wake up*. Isn't that amazing? Peter, James, and John were all asleep in the midst of a great time of worship. When the sower sowed the seed, man slept (Matthew 13:24). When Jesus prayed in Gethsemane, the disciples slept (Matthew 26:40). While Paul preached in Greece, Eutychus slept (Acts 20:7–12). Today, the modern church has drifted off into a deep sleep, and the world, flesh and devil have been at work. Jesus told the church at Sardis, "Wake up."

We need to *grow up*. Peter and the brothers showed some real immaturity. Even after he woke up, leave it to Peter to say the wrong thing. Jesus was showing His glory and speaking of His coming death, but Peter wanted to stay on the mountain and enter a building program. It was as if Peter was saying, "Lord, let's not go back down; let's stay here. Don't go to the cross and die." Folks, we need to grow up.

We need to *listen up*. In the silence of this moment, a voice came from the cloud and said, "This is my beloved Son, listen to Him." The law and the prophets were only partial expressions, but now we have the final word; listen to Him. It reminds me of the opening verses of Hebrews: "God, after He spoke long ago to the fathers in the prophets in many portions and in many ways, in these last days has spoken to us in His Son" (1:1–2a). This event made such an impression on Peter that he wrote about it years later.

For we did not follow cleverly devised tales when we made known to you the power and coming of our Lord Jesus Christ, but we were eyewitnesses of His majesty. For when He received honor and glory from God the Father, such an utterance as this was made to Him by the Majestic Glory, "This is My beloved Son with whom I am well-pleased"—and we ourselves heard this utterance made from heaven when we were with Him on the holy mountain. (2 Peter 1:16–18)

The Departure from Jerusalem (Luke 9:31)

Jesus is joined on the mount by Moses and Elijah. Yes, that Moses and that Elijah. One was part of the law; the other, the prophets. Both were great leaders and spokesmen for God, and they were speaking (talking) with Jesus. I've often wondered what all was said. "Hey Moses, that bush on fire; that was me. Yes, Elijah, I sent the fire, and I drove the chariot. And Moses … why did you hit the rock? That was me. Did you like the manna and quail? Pretty cool, huh? Hey Elijah, you like what I did with the oil? What about the dead boy?"

Yes, some of these things may have been discussed, but we do know they spoke of His exodus (departure). This would have included Jesus's ultimate death, resurrection, and ascension. Jesus always understood why He came and what His purpose was here.

Though a different Greek word, the English word *departure* is used elsewhere in scripture, and it represents going from one place to another, to loosen the moorings of a ship and to sail on, for a military group to break camp and leave for another place, to unyoke an animal, or to be loosed from sickness and disease. These ideas further illustrate much of what our Lord was facing and accomplishing in His death.

The Glory of Jehovah (Luke 9:34)

It had been six hundred years since anyone in the land of Israel had seen the Shekinah, the glory of God. But while Peter was speaking, "a cloud appeared and began to overshadow them" (v. 34). The Shekinah was the visible presence of God. This presence hovered over the children of Israel after the Exodus (Exodus 13:21). It was seen by Moses (Exodus 33–34). It appeared over the tabernacle (Exodus 40:34, 35), and it filled the temple (2 Chronicles 7:1–3). However, in 2 Chronicles 9:3, 6, the glory departs (Ichabod).

Now, after a six-hundred-year absence, the glory cloud was back.

Not only does this moment point back, it gazes forward, to the coming day of His glory. Jesus is the Glory.

What a day this was, and after it ended, "Jesus was found alone" (9:36). Jesus is the far greater one ... the preeminent one ... the one and only.

"Listen to Him" (9:35).

Exploration Guide

1. What is a memorable mountaintop experience from your life? What do you recall about this time?
2. What is significant about who accompanied Jesus to the mountain and who showed up?
3. When you hear "metamorphosis," what do you think of?
4. What is significant of the departure of Moses, Elijah, and Jesus from earth?
5. Discuss the glory of God throughout the scripture.
6. Read Colossians 1:18. Discuss this verse in light of Peter's words on the mount.

Mount Hermon (Caesarea Philippi)

Matthew 16

There is something medicinal or therapeutic about going to the mountains. I grew up in northwest Alabama, so we knew nothing about mountains. Wait, there is an Indian mound there that school groups visit. When I first saw it years ago, I wasn't very impressed.

But Alabama church groups have been getting away to the mountains of East Tennessee or the ski slopes of West Virginia and North Carolina for years. In fact, I'm not sure you can have a youth event or Bible conference today that isn't connected to Gatlinburg. As I said, medicinal and therapeutic; maybe even spiritual.

The same is true in the northern reaches of the Holy Land in a place called Dan (or Banias), which is at the base of Mount Hermon (actually located in modern-day Syria). After spending time in the hot and barren wilderness of Israel, which is what much of the land is, when you come north to Dan, it always feels refreshing.

The first time I traveled to Dan, I was quite amazed at the greenery and lushness of the area. Trees, crops, nature, springs, rivers, and even ski slopes (no, that's not a typo). If you've ever been on a mountain hike with shade and trees and a mountain stream flowing around you, that's the idea of Dan. It's a place where locals go to hike, picnic, or just relax.

Dan is the northernmost spot in Israel. Dan, as you recall, was the name of Jacob's fifth son, and this city became best known as the northern extreme of Israel, as mentioned in Judges 20:1, "From Dan to Beersheba."

Today, instead of escaping to the ski slopes in close proximity to Banias, let's learn some history and theology from this famous but often confusing text.

The Location

This site has had a variety of names through the years. In the time of Joshua, the area was known as Baal Gad (Joshua 11:16–17), named for the fertility god Baal. A temple indicates this was a center for Baal worship. After the conquest led by Alexander the Great, this area came under Greek rule and influence. At this time, the area was called Paneas, after the Greek god Pan. Pan was the god of nature, flocks, herds, and shepherds. After Paneas was conquered by Rome, the city was placed under the authority of Herod the Great, who was then the king. Herod built a white marble temple there, and some of its remains are still visible. He dedicated this temple and the area to the Roman Emperor Augustus. After Herod's death, the area was passed on to his son Phillip, who ruled the area from 4 BC until his own death forty years later. Herod Phillip rebuilt the city and renamed it for Tiberias and himself, thus the name Caesarea Philippi.

Because of the history of idolatrous Baal and Pan worship, this area became a real haven for sinful activity. Caesarea was viewed as the sin city of Israel, in the way many today view Las Vegas or New Orleans. People worshipped Baal, Pan, Caesar, nature, you name it, through wild parties and sexual orgies.

So isn't it interesting that Jesus leads His disciples on a thirty-plus-mile journey from Bethesda to a site like this, surrounded by much temptation, to find out where their heart really is? The worst of places was about to bring out the very best of Peter.

The Lord

Once on-site, perhaps with the backdrop of an idolatrous temple with pagan worship and worshippers nearby, Jesus proposed a question: "Who do people say that the Son of Man is?" (Matthew 16:13). Maybe it was more like, "Boys, what are you hearing? What are people beginning to say about what they hear Me say and see Me do?" Because of what He asked them and where it was asked, it's likely He wanted to see if they truly understood and were committed. It's a good question for us too.

What were the throngs of people saying? Now, for over two years, these twelve men had listened and learned, witnessed His actions, and watched people's responses. What were they hearing? Was He just a *prophet* who made bold declarations? Was He a *physician* who could cure, heal, and even raise the dead? Was He a *philosopher* who spoke with eloquence, authority, and insight? Was He a *prankster* who was involved in magical acts and deceptive practices? Or was He much more than that?

Jesus then gets personal and pointed, asking, "But who do you say that I am?" Of course, it would be Peter who speaks up. Not only is Simon the "leader" of the pack, he is normally seen as the spokesman. "You are the Christ [the Messiah], the Son of the living God." After all he had seen and heard, after two years of ministry and miracles, after long walks and late-night conversations, Peter is now convinced, and he's convincing. "Jesus, you are the long-awaited King, you are the Messiah, you are Lord, and you alone are to be worshipped and served." I too am convinced of that. Are you?

The Lie

Much has been said of Jesus's reply to Simon in v. 18: "I also say to you that you are Peter and upon this rock I will build My church; and the gates of Hades will not overpower it." In responding to him, Jesus makes a play on words that is crucial to understand.

The name Peter is *Petros*, which is best translated as "pebble" or "small stone." Petros describes a shifting or moving rock, more like a piece of gravel or sand. This is not the type of foundation anyone would want to build on. Rather, Jesus says He will build His church on the rock, or petra. This word describes a solid rock or foundation stone. Peter's statement of Jesus being the Messiah is the foundation stone that the church is built on. My hope is built on nothing less than Jesus's blood and righteousness. I dare not trust the sweetest frame but wholly lean on Jesus's name. Jesus Christ, the Lord, is our solid rock.

Sadly, many in our world believe a flawed theology that makes more of Simon Peter than was ever intended. Peter was a disciple, a fisherman, and a sinner. He never was a pope and never was destined to be. I'd hate to think that my church, eh, my salvation, was built on a mere man who in a few short weeks would react in anger, deny the Lord, curse, swear, and abandon ship. Such was the life of one "shifting stone."

The Link

There may be another reason Jesus led His guys to Caesarea Philippi and to this site. An indication may be seen in v. 18: "and the gates of Hades." Jesus asked this famed question and gave His response in front of the large temple in Caesarea Philippi, located at the opening of a massive cave believed by some ancients to be the entrance to hell. So this area is called the Gates of Hell. Through time, as many as seven temples were built on this spot.

Much worship in Christ's time was to the god Pan. To please or appease this god, people would throw their children into the mouth of the cave, down into the water. If the child sank and drowned, the god was satisfied, and no further sacrifice was necessary. If the child floated or somehow survived, then more human sacrifices were needed. What an abomination!

In the face of this idolatry and in front of this cave/temple, Jesus wanted to find out just what His followers believed and how committed they really were. Perhaps you've been to Caesarea Philippi or you're headed there soon, but you don't have to go to this location to begin some real soul-searching. Who do you say that Jesus is?

Don't listen to the lies of the world or look to mere men for help or direction; Jesus Christ is the Messiah, and He alone will save us and satisfy us.

1. Do you have a favorite mountain getaway? Why is it special? What do you enjoy about it?
2. What does "Dan to Beersheba" mean?
3. How are Jesus's words to Peter often misinterpreted? Why is this so wrong?
4. What does the word "Hades" mean? Why is that word significant in this location?
5. God has promised to build His church. What part are we to play in this matter?

Valley of Hinnom

Luke 16

We are viewing all types of mountains and valleys in our study. Some are special and spectacular; some are serious. Some destinations are delightful and great; this one is destructive. Going to or through some create shouts of joy; at Hinnom are cries of anguish and screams of fear. Today, we will look at the Valley of Hinnom.

The word *hinnom* (or *gehenna*) is a translation of a word meaning "the valley of whining" or "valley of lamenting." This valley is located just south of Jerusalem. When you walk through the current Dung Gate, you are looking out toward the Valley of Hinnom.

As you look over this valley, you see some homes, a church, and some vegetation. This view is dramatically different from what one would have seen in Christ's time. Scripture tells us about the child sacrifices that happened in this valley to the gods of Baal and Moloch. This location became a garbage dump; all the city waste was taken there, thus the Dung Gate. Because of this, there would have been fires burning here around the clock. These perpetual fires were at the root of why the word gehenna is one of the words translated "hell." When Jesus spoke of hell being a place of torture, fire, and burning, His audience would have understood.

Historians also believe this to be the location of where Judas Iscariot went out to hang himself. We know here was the field that the priests bought with the thirty pieces of silver (blood money) Judas was given and then returned. That field was named Hakeldama, the Field of Blood, and it is home to a modern-day church/monastery. Imagine living or worshiping over such a location, with such a history.

When modern groups of tourists stand on the Mount of Olives and look toward the Old City of Jerusalem, it is very easy to see the Valley of Hinnom to the left. As one stands at the lookout above the dungeon in Caiaphas's house, you can clearly see this valley.

It may seem strange to visit such a valley. If you were to visit me in my hometown, I wouldn't take you to the city dump for an afternoon of activity. However, the Valley of Hinnom is not just important for what happened there in history but rather because of what it represents: the place called hell. This is not a subject we like to talk about or discuss, but truly we must.

In Luke 16, Jesus tells a story that most believe is a parable, an earthly story with a heavenly or spiritual meaning. (Note: Some pastors say this story is an actual literal event, because of the use of a proper name Lazarus. However, every other feature of this text fits the pattern of a parable.) This is a story about two fellows, two funerals, and two futures. Lazarus dies and goes to Abraham's bosom (heaven), while the rich man also dies and descends into hell. It's quite a story and worth taking the time to read. One can glean much about this place of destruction for those who don't know our Lord.

Because this subject matter is avoided by many or written off as mere myth or legend, I feel it crucial to answer some simple but serious questions about this valley and about hell.

Why I Believe in a Literal Hell

Many people, even ministers, try to avoid this topic or explain it away. They joke about it, mock those who believe it, or even ridicule the idea. I'll be honest with you: You can ignore this subject all you want, but it will not ignore you. We are warned about this place over 160 times in scripture; almost half of these warnings are uttered by none other than our Lord. So the most compassionate and tenderhearted person who ever lived constantly warned His audience of the real place called hell. Listen to some of the passages:

But I say to you that everyone who is angry with his brother shall be guilty before the court; and whoever says to his brother, "You good-for-nothing," shall be guilty before the supreme court; and whoever says, "You fool," shall be guilty enough to go into the fiery hell. (Matthew 5:22)

If your eye causes you to stumble, pluck it out and throw it from you. It is better for you to enter life with one eye, than to have two eyes and be cast into the fiery hell. (Matthew 18:9)

And the smoke of their torment goes up forever and ever; they have no rest day and night, those who worship the beast and his image, and whoever receives the mark of his name. (Revelation 14:11)

And if anyone's name was not found written in the book of life, he was thrown into the lake of fire. (Revelation 20:15)

But for the cowardly and unbelieving and abominable and murderers and immoral persons and sorcerers and idolaters and all liars, their part will be in the lake that burns with fire and brimstone, which is the second death. (Revelation 21:8)

In addition to what the Bible says about hell, and that is enough, when I look at what Jesus went through in paying my sin debt, His becoming sin for me, I'm reminded that God takes sin and judgment very seriously. I would have no respect for any Father who would allow His Son to go through such anguish and torture without just cause, nor would you. But Jesus went *through* hell so you don't have to go *to* hell.

What the Bible Teaches about This Place

Many verses teach us what we know about this place. Let me point out a few:

Darkness. "And cast him into outer darkness" (Matthew 25:30). One of the plagues of Egypt was a darkness so intense it could be felt. I remember when Michelle and I were dating. I was driving across a bridge into her city, and as I approached Colbert County, Alabama, there was not one light on. Something had happened to the neighborhood's power; one of the Tennessee Valley Authority's transformers had blown. For a bit, every light in that part of the city was not working; it was eerie, scary, and I could feel it. Jesus said that hell will be like that, just worse.

Horrific. In this place, there is "weeping and gnashing of teeth"

(Matthew 22:13). One can only imagine the horror, cries, screams, anxiety, and fear experienced there.

Fiery. "Where the fire is not quenched" (Mark 9:48). "I am in agony in this flame" (Luke 16:24). "The smoke of their torment ascends up forever and ever" (Revelation 14:11). When you compile all New Testament texts, you read about the lake of fire, burning fire, unquenchable fire, flames of fire, eternal fire, and fire and brimstone. This is not a pretty picture.

Agony. "Forever and ever" (Revelation 14:11). One of the real tragedies of hell is not that people burn; it's that they don't burn up. Annihilation is not taught in the Bible. In fact, just the opposite is. Lost humanity will suffer in torment forever and ever. (Stop and let that sink in for a moment.)

Regret. "Son, remember" (Luke 16:25). This parable teaches me that those in hell will have the capacity to remember for all of eternity that sermon, song, or service; perhaps it's that friend's prayer or a parent's plea. Forever etched in one's mind are the opportunities shunned and the choices made.

Separation. "A great chasm fixed" (Luke 16:26). Think of what this means. Separated from the Lord, His redeemed people, and all that is good and worthwhile, forever. This great chasm is fixed in place, and it will not and cannot be changed.

These items and so many more not only describe the place called hell, but they should provoke us to action toward the lost and win them before it is eternally too late.

Who Will Spend Eternity in Hell? (Revelation 21:8)

Anyone and everyone who has not trusted our Lord and come to understand His grace is going to hell. In fact, listen to John the Revelator's words: "But the cowardly and unbelieving and abominable and murderers and immoral persons and sorcerers and idolaters and all liars, will have their part in the lake of fire and brimstone, which is the second death" (Revelation 21:8). That's a bad list, no doubt, but it begins with people in fear and those who don't believe.

In fact, Jesus said that the majority, most people, are going to end up in hell. That's hard to wrap our minds around in a universalistic world, but it's true. Few are going to heaven, and many are going to hell (Matthew 7:13–14).

How Can We Avoid Going to Hell?

While it's true most people will end up in hell, it's also true they don't have to. All those who come to the Lord Jesus, repent of their sin, and place their faith in Him and His work of grace and redemption, can escape hell and go to heaven. If that's a commitment you have never made, I urge you to do so today. Right now.

You will learn about many valleys in this book, and at some point in your life, you will go through some (maybe not physically, but spiritually or emotionally). You'll find some giants in Elah or some troubles in Achor, or you'll come to your own death and its shadowy valley, but you don't have to ever enter Hinnom and all it entails, if you've come to know our Lord. May it be so for you.

Exploration Guide

1. Have you ever been to your city's dump? What images do you recall from being there?
2. What is the difference in the words we use to translate the word *hell*?
3. What is a parable? Is this story parabolic? Why or why not?
4. Of the items the Bible teaches about hell, which of these is most alarming to you? Why?
5. Will people really go to hell for eternity?
6. How do you escape going to hell?

Mount of Olives

Matthew 21, 24; Acts 1

I love standing on the Mount of Olives, looking over the Kidron Valley and toward the Old City of Jerusalem. This mountain was very important to Jesus and in the lives of His disciples. When you stop at one of the many teaching spots, it is always quite thrilling to imagine what happened where you stand and Who walked there.

As you look west toward the city, the panoramic view is stunning. If you look to the south and begin to pan right, you'll see Hinnom, the City of David, the rooftop of Bathsheba (not really), Caiaphas's house, Old City Wall, Mosque of Omar, Dome of the Rock, Church of the Holy Sepulcher, Eastern Gate, Gethsemane, Absalom's tomb, and three large cemeteries. There are thousands of graves of Christians, Jews, and Muslims, all buried with their feet toward the Temple Mount and only meters away from the Walled City. Each group believes something significant is yet to happen here, and they're right.

As you gaze upon this sight, you are overwhelmed by the history before your eyes, from several thousand years back to at least a thousand years forward.

Jesus spent a lot of time on this mountain. From here, He would train and teach His disciples, go to Gethsemane to pray, head down to Bethany or Jericho, and answer some questions and calm some hearts. From here, He would leave for the cross and later for His heavenly home.

The Olivet Descent (Matthew 21:1–11)

It was from the Mount of Olives that Jesus would begin the route of His Palm Sunday parade into Jerusalem. Today, groups can walk down this steep incline on the ancient roadway that has been paved over. This road begins at the top of the Mount of Olives and winds down toward the bottom in the Kidron Valley. Merchants often line this roadway; some have very picturesque donkeys you can get your photograph with (for a fee, of course).

We often read Matthew 21 on this descent and perhaps enact its narrative. "Hosanna ... Hosanna ... Blessed is He who comes in the name of the Lord." I can hear the mobs, "Tell them to be quiet, hush." To which Jesus, seeing all the dead stones on the graves, replies, "I tell you if they keep silent, these very stones will cry out." It changes how you see the passage.

As you read Matthew 21, there are several things that are happening:

- Scripture is being fulfilled (v. 5: Zechariah 9:9).
- Scripture is being quoted (v. 9: Psalm 119:26).
- Scripture is being missed. While quoting Psalm 118:26, they overlook 118:22–23.

It's a great reminder that just because someone can quote a biblical text, that doesn't mean that their sermon is correct or their heart is right. Celebration is one thing; consecration is another.

The Olivet Discourse (Matthew 24:3–25:46)

Though I've pastored for almost four decades, preached thousands of sermons, and have multiple degrees, I'm certainly no theologian or expert in eschatology, the study in last things. Really, I don't care what your viewpoint is on the rapture or the tribulation, on judgments or the millennium. For many years, I've been taught (and taught) end-times issues from a pre-tribulation/pre-Millennial framework. I believe and hope I'm right. Honestly, if you are persuaded otherwise, **you** should hope I'm right too.

But for our purposes here, let me just say that I've had good and godly professors, pastors, and parishioners agree and disagree with my belief, and that's okay. They're entitled to be wrong. Today, I'm not on the program committee; I serve in the Welcome Center. I don't care if you're "pre, post, or A." When it comes to the Millennial Reign of Christ, I'm a "Pan-man"; it will all pan out.

All kidding aside, it will benefit you greatly to get some theological handles on this issue and be able to defend your beliefs. So many people today can tell you what they believe, but they don't know why.

This discourse seeks to answer two key questions the disciples asked Jesus (v. 3) after His comment, "Do you see these things? [temple buildings] Truly I say to you, not one stone here will be left upon another, which will not be torn down" (Matthew 24:1–2).

Once they exit the Temple Mount area, pass through the Kidron Valley, and get back to the Mount of Olives, the disciples ask Jesus privately, "Tell us, when will these things happen, and what will be the sign of your coming?" In the verses that follow, Jesus begins to answer these questions.

As you read chapters 24 and 25, you'll learn things about the tribulation, Abomination of Desolation (fulfillment of Daniel 9), the rapture, the Second Coming of Christ, judgments, rewards, and the Millennial Reign of Christ. Regardless of the lens you choose to look through in your application, we can all agree that this is a fascinating text with much to learn and apply.

The key is "be on the alert" (24:42, 25:13) and to "be ready" (24:44).

The Olivet Departure (Acts 1:9–12)

Yes, there are many things we can't say with complete certainty, but there are many others that we can, and we shall, and we must. It was from this majestic mountain that Jesus ascended to heaven and will come again one day.

His Removal (9)

What a sight it must have been when our Lord was carried away to glory. After His death and burial, then Jesus *arose*. He *appeared* to many; He *authorized* His disciples to "go into all the world"; and then He returned from Galilee to Olivet to *ascend*. Just like that, Jesus had gone from Galilee to Jerusalem, from one favorite spot to another, and the glory cloud of God came by to transport Jesus home.

His Return (11)

It's to this same location that Jesus will one day return. That same cloud that took Him away will bring Him back. In fact, wouldn't it be great to start singing now:

The King is Coming.
The King is Coming.
Praise God, He's Coming for me.

Long ago, the prophet Zechariah saw this moment and wrote, "In that day His feet will stand on the Mount of Olives, which is in front of Jerusalem on the east; and the Mount of Olives will be split in its middle from east to west by a very large valley" (14:4).

Child of God, we must all long for and look for our Lord's return. In fact, we were taught to pray, "Thy kingdom come on earth." Like the disciples who watched Him being taken away, we need to anticipate His glorious return.

Maranatha! Come, Lord.

Exploration Guide

1. Where is the Mount of Olives located?
2. What familiar places are close by this mount? Discuss.
3. What do we mean by the "Olivet discourse"? What was this about?
4. What is it we are to be alert for and to be ready for?
5. What most excites you about our Lord's return?
6. What should we be doing as we await Jesus's return?

Mount Golgotha (Calvary)

Matthew 27

Every business today has a website, a logo, and a mission statement. In fact, if you don't have one, and a sharp one at that, you'll be left out or run over. Sports teams have a special color and their own brand. Some families have a coat of arms to identify them and their ancestors. The point is everyone and everything is noticed by their own emblem. The cross is the emblem of Christianity.

Honestly, what we wear today would have produced questions or raised eyebrows in the first century. The cross was a symbol of a cruel form of punishment and death. We would roll our eyes if we saw people today adorned with a hangman's noose, electric chair, or firing squad, but they too are such symbols. But the cross in the life of a believer is a reminder and focal point of our faith. It's where "the one who knew no sin became sin for us so that we might become His righteous ones" (2 Corinthians 5:21). The cross is more than a logo, emblem, or calling card; the cross was where the Son of God died for the sins of the world, your sins and mine.

Though I'm not so certain this cross was "on a hill far away," believers and many enquirers alike understand the idea behind a mount on which there were three crosses. In fact, on a recent drive through Kentucky and West Virginia, Michelle and I counted dozens of times that we spotted crosses on a hill. People of faith do this because they are aware of the biblical account of Jesus's death on a cross between the crosses of two thieves.

When you visit the modern city of Jerusalem, you can actually see a few places which are believed to have been Mount Calvary. One place is currently inside the walls of the Church of the Holy Sepulcher. Since the fourth century, many have believed this to be the place of Jesus's death, burial, and resurrection. Today, hundreds of thousands of tourists and pilgrims visit the site, pray their prayers, and light their candles. It may very well be the actual location, but honestly, my heart cringes every time I visit. It has become a place of religious idolatry.

Outside the current wall and above the Garden of Gethsemane is another "scalped hill" some think is Calvary or Golgotha. This view lacks historical or biblical evidence.

For many evangelicals, including myself, our heart seems to be drawn to a fairly recent find just outside the current wall of the Old City called "Gordon's Calvary," named after the Englishman who discovered it in the early 1900s. It has all the markings. There is a noticeable skull hill and a roadway; it's part of Mount Moriah, it's outside the city, north of the altar, and there is a neighboring garden, wine press, and tomb. And frankly, it fits nicely into our mental image of what we believe and what our heart says.

Again, where this event happened is not the crucial point; that it happened, why it happened, and what it accomplished, is.

The word *Calvary* is from the Greek word *Kranion,* or "skull." This is an interpretation from the Aramaic *golgotha,* the place of the skull(s). Our English word comes from the Latin word *calvaria.* One legend claims that when David returned from defeating Goliath, he went to Jerusalem (1 Samuel 17:54) and buried the giant's head at Skull Hill, or Calvary. That's conjecture at best, but it is an interesting note.

Mount Calvary is the basis of countless sermons and songs. Many pastors have waxed eloquent on this subject, and ancient hymn writers and modern songwriters have all weighed in. Calvary is also a place for some sayings or statements. Seven different lines are recorded in the Gospels that were uttered by Jesus while on the cross:

"Father, forgive them, for they know not what they do" (Luke 23:34).
"Today, you will be with me in Paradise" (Luke 23:43).
"Behold thy Son ... Behold Thy mother" (John 19:26, 27).

"Why hast Thou forsaken Me?" (Matthew 27:46).

"I thirst" (John 19:28).

"It is finished" (John 19:30).

"Into Thy hands I commend my Spirit" (Luke 23:46).

However, today, we are not going to worry ourselves with where this event occurred or when it happened or even why. I want us to view some of the "what." What happened after Jesus died that was so miraculous that Matthew couldn't help but record it. Many preachers have called these events the Five Mighty Miracles of Calvary (Spurgeon actually wrote of seven). Let's view these five.

The Sun (Matthew 27:45)

Liberal commentators have tried to say this didn't happen, that the darkness was due to a sandstorm or an eclipse of the sun. This was no eclipse, for it was Passover, the time of a new moon. Astronomically speaking, an eclipse at this time would have been impossible. This darkness was indeed supernatural, perhaps like that in Exodus.

The prophet Habakkuk writes of our God, "Your eyes are too pure to approve evil, and you cannot look on wickedness with favor" (Habakkuk 1:13a). From noon until three o'clock, it was midnight in the middle of the day. Why? For "Jesus bore our sin in His body on the cross," and the "one who knew no sin became sin." As this happens, God placed a funeral drapery over all the earth; creation mourned in silence and darkness.

The Veil (Matthew 27:50–51a)

The earth was dark for three hours, and then, after Jesus's death, the next four events happen in rapid succession. Now that sin was atoned for and Jesus's payment was final, the darkness lifted, and the "veil of the temple is torn in two"; we now have access, not an obstruction.

The Jewish temple has a series of walls and courts. Non-Jews could go into the "court of the gentiles" but no farther. Jewish women could enter the "court of the women" but no farther. Jewish men could go farther, but only the priest could go into the Holy Place. Beyond that was another wall, a veil. Only the High Priest could go beyond the veil, until now. The writer of Hebrews speaks of this moment: "By a new and living way which He inaugurated for us through the Veil, that is, His flesh." Because of what Jesus did, you and I now have access to God every moment of every day. You don't have to go through a pope, priest, prophet, or preacher. You have access through the work of Jesus Christ. So come boldly before His throne of grace (Hebrews 4:16).

The Earthquake (Matthew 27:51b)

At the same time the veil was being torn, there was a very strong earthquake. This earthquake was not a coincidence; rather, it was God's divine punctuation mark at the end of judgment. Rocks drenched with our Lord's blood lifted up their voices in protest as we crucified our Maker.

Do you recall when Jesus entered Jerusalem on Palm Sunday and the people cheered? Some said to Jesus, "Tell them to be quiet." Jesus replies, "If these become silent even the stones will cry out" (Luke 19:40). Now, man is silent, nature is silent, all the world is silent, and the rocks cry out. When all the others quit Him, abandoned Him, fled Him, forsook Him, hid from Him, or walked out on Him, the rocks did split.

The Tombs (Matthew 27:52–53)

I don't even pretend to know all that this event means. I don't know who these former dead people were. I don't know where they went or what they did or even how they looked, nor do you. I do know that this amazing situation was a foretaste of the day when all the graves of all the redeemed are opened, and they come forth. Jesus is "the resurrection and the life," and one day, we'll be singing, "Ain't no grave gonna hold this body down."

The Centurion (Matthew 27:54)

Have you ever been in the front row of a play or concert? This soldier was on the front row of one of the world's greatest events (the other being the angel at the grave on Easter morning). Could it be that one who was part of the fight was now declaring his faith?

What courage. In spite of his peers, the moment the great crowd gathered at Golgotha, this soldier had the boldness to say, "Truly this was the Son of God."

What a confession. No, this one verse doesn't necessarily prove his salvation or his part in God's plan, but it is a great declaration of the deity of Christ and a great recognition of the Father's work. I personally believe we will meet this man one day in heaven. Can you just imagine him, the thief, Jesus, and the disciple who wrote about it, all talking about that *Good* Friday?

The real question is, do you have the same courage, and will you make the same confession? If so, one day, you'll join all the others on the front row of eternity. Glory.

Exploration Guide

1. When you think of Mount Calvary and Golgotha, what images come to your mind?
2. In what ways had the Romans perfected this cruel form of capital punishment?
3. Discuss the Lord's seven recorded statements while on the cross. What is the meaning of each?
4. All five miracles listed are amazing. Which of them is most interesting to you? Why?
5. What was the purpose of the veil in the temple? Why is its tearing so "disruptive"? So "glorious"?

Mount of Temple

Matthew 24, Revelation 11

There is no city in the world quite like Jerusalem. It's not necessarily large or spacious. There are no skyscrapers, waterfalls, or space needles. No, this city is amazing for other reasons. Many other reasons.

Jerusalem is home to three great religions. Of course, it's home to Judaism and Christianity, but it is also home to Islam. Today, in a nation of almost 9 million people, most are Jews. Then there are Muslims. And lastly, there are a few Christians. Of this third group, most are CINO (Christian in name only). Best estimates say there are around five thousand evangelicals in the land, a minority among minorities.

Many people believe Jerusalem is the center of the world. In fact, Judaism teaches that the Garden of Eden was here and that beneath the Dome of the Rock is where God first began to create the world. One cannot be certain of that, but so much more of this city's history is easy to follow and learn about. Such is true with the Temple Mount.

Many older towns in America have a courthouse in the center of town, usually around a square. Around this square are churches, businesses, and restaurants. This is not only the center of the city; it's the center of activity, commerce, and socializing. Such was the case in Jerusalem on and around the Temple Mount area. There would have always been a buzz about the place; there still is.

The Temple Mount is exactly what the name says, it is the mount or foundation on which the ancient temples were built. In a sense, this is a "mount upon a mount" since it is on top of Mount Moriah. As such, this mount has implications in the past, present, and future.

The Past

Not only is Israel God's land, but Jerusalem is His chosen city. 2 Chronicles 6:6 says, "But I have chosen Jerusalem that My name might be there." As such, God has always put His signature on this location.

Perhaps this was the original location of the Garden of Eden. We can't say for certain, but many other events have happened here. Of those, you should be aware of the following:

- Abraham took Isaac to be offered as a sacrifice here (Genesis 22:1–14).
- David built an altar here and may have housed his tabernacle on this site (1 Chronicles 21:18, 2 Chronicles 3:1).
- Solomon built the first temple on this location in 587 BC. It's awesome to read God's glory coming down and filling this place (2 Chronicles 5:11–14).
- Temple of Zerubbabel. After the decree of Cyrus in Ezra (536 BC), the foundation was begun in 520. The second temple was smaller than Solomon's and less sumptuous. When it was completed, the old men wept (Ezra 6:16).
- Temple of Herod. This was a reconstruction of the second temple. Herod's masterpiece was begun in 20 BC and stood until its destruction by Titus of Rome in AD 70. This was the temple where Jesus would have come many times.

As one views the Temple Mount through these many years, it is easy to see dedication, disappointment, and destruction. The prophet Haggai writes, "'The latter glory of the house will be greater than the former,' says the Lord of hosts, 'and in this place I will give peace,' declares the Lord" (Haggai 2:9). I can't help but think that the Lord spoke of Herod's time and beyond.

The Present

Jerusalem is not just geographically the center of the world; in many ways, it's also the center geopolitically. Hundreds, thousands, and yes, even millions of people visit this land, more specifically this city, annually. According to the *Jerusalem Post*, a record-breaking 4.55 million tourists came in 2019. This is an increase of 1 million in just the last two years.

A.) **A Place of History**

People from every corner of the world come to Jerusalem for various reasons. Some may not even know why. "It's just the history," they say. I remind you, history is really His story.

At the Temple Mount, there is much you can see. You can join others in praying at the Western Wall, tour the recently excavated Kotel Tunnels, view Robinson's Arch, or even stop for a time of devotion on the Southern Steps. At almost any point, the area around the mount is filled with tourists, prayers, locals, and armed Israeli soldiers. You'll often overhear music and singing from a bar mitzvah, that time when a Jewish boy comes of age. There is no place like this in all the world.

B.) **A Place of Hostility**

Almost daily, there are minor uprisings between the different cultures, sects, groups, and even travelers coming to the mount. To access this area, you have to go through a checkpoint similar to that of airport security. In our world, this has become all too common, but for some people, these checkpoints are offensive and intrusive, so it raises their emotions. Once through security, you can go to the Western Wall or actually access the Temple Mount at certain times of the day. When one group believes the area inhabited by another group belongs to them, well, you can imagine the friction.

Though I've personally never seen any issues at this site, you'd think by listening to the modern news media that World War III breaks out every day.

The Future

The activity of this place has happened, it is happening, and it is yet to happen. God is not done working in or visiting Jerusalem. Evidently, there are two other times this mount will house a temple. One will be built during the tribulation times. The temple will fulfill the Abomination of Desolation prophecy of Daniel 9 and Matthew 24. John also writes of this in Revelation 11.

The Millennial Temple referenced in Ezekiel 40–48 and Revelation 20 will be constructed and coronated by our King, the Lord Jesus. This temple will last for a thousand years, as the word *millennial* means.

Finally, that great Christmas carol, "Joy to the World," can be sung with meaning:

Joy to the World,
the Lord is come.
Let Earth receive her King.

He rules the world with Truth and Grace
and makes the nations prove
the Glories of His Righteousness
and Wonders of His Love.
(Handel/Watts)

In 1969, Neal Armstrong was on Apollo 11 and became the first man to ever walk on the moon. Surely you recall, "That's one small step for man, and one giant leap for mankind." Just a few years ago, Armstrong was visiting Jerusalem and was climbing the Southern Steps to the Temple Mount. When he realized the significance of this place and knew without a doubt His Lord had walked there, he replied, "Never have I been so deeply moved. I walked on the moon, but nothing compares to this location in Jerusalem and on these steps." It was a holy moment.

I've never walked on the moon, but I have been on these steps, and I have to tell you, I agree. Reader, if you can, visit this city and this mount.

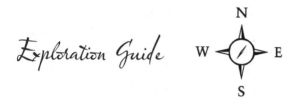

Exploration Guide

1. Discuss the three religions having an interest in Jerusalem and in the Temple Mount.
2. What do you know about each temple period?
3. Why did men weep at the sight of the second temple?
4. Read Haggai 2:9. What great truths are recorded here?
5. What is the Abomination of Desolation? When will this take place?

Mount Zion

Hebrews 12

No matter how many times I've done it, the drive from Ben Gurion Airport in Tel Aviv to Jerusalem is always majestic. Naturally, some people in your group may be new to the Holy Land. So as you begin to make the short drive up to the holy city, people's eyes are opened, and their sense of awareness is heightened. I can almost read their minds: *I can't believe I'm here, my Lord's land, where He walked. Wow.* I know they think that because I still do as well.

Normally, this roadway is filled with locals and tourists, business leaders and pilgrims, students and theologians, all moving in cars, vans, motorbikes, and buses. The congestion creates a naturally slow pace and allows you to begin taking in the sights and scenes of Israel. Jerusalem is built on a mountain and surrounded by mountains, so naturally you begin to go up in elevation. On many occasions, our Bible speaks of going up to Jerusalem, and you do.

Mount Zion is a name synonymous with Jerusalem. Originally, Mount Zion referred to a rocky ridge that was adjacent to and ran along the Kidron Valley. Later, the word was broadened to include the entire western ridge of Jerusalem, and finally, it means the entire Old City.

Zion is a transliteration of some Greek and Hebrew words meaning "the hill." The hill in reference was this portion of Jerusalem that David conquered from the Jebusites (2 Samuel 5); it became known as the "city of David" (2 Samuel 5:7). Here, King David had his palace, threshing floor, and an altar. Interestingly, this area is a rather recent find; the excavations here are ongoing. The area is just outside the current city walls.

Mount Zion (or just Zion) has a threefold significance in the scriptures. It speaks of Israel's past as David's city (2 Samuel 5, 1 Chronicles 11, Psalm 2, Isaiah 2) or the church's future, in a prophetic sense as the Millennial City or the capital of Israel in the Kingdom Age (Isaiah 1, 2, 4; Joel 3; Zechariah 1, 8). It's worth noting that in the last few years, the American Embassy was moved from Tel Aviv to Jerusalem. It also reminds us of the believer's eternity, for it is called the Heavenly City of the New Jerusalem (Hebrews 12, Revelation 21–22). Mount Zion's past and future are quite busy.

There are many Bible references that speak of Mount Zion, but most significantly are the fifteen psalms known as Psalms of Ascent or Degrees. There is a variety of opinions as to what the ascent or degree really implies. Is it a musical idea, meaning a higher chord or key? Does the idea of degrees connect them in some way to King Hezekiah? Do these psalms speak of the stages we would take on the journey back to the Promised Land and Holy City? Were they used in reference to the stolen Ark of the Covenant being brought under David's control? Maybe there is a connection of the fifteen psalms to the fifteen stops between the court of women and that of men; a psalm is chanted at each stop. Really, we don't know.

Most theologians and teachers think they are simply pilgrim songs sung by the throngs of people on their way to Jerusalem for one of the festivals. One can almost hear the families of people rejoicing or celebrating Jehovah God's faithfulness. "I will lift up my eyes to the mountains … my help comes from the Lord" (Psalm 121:1, 2). Can't you just imagine Mary, Joseph, and Jesus singing out? Jesus may have told His disciples as they approached Jerusalem, "Let me teach you a psalm my parents taught me."

These fifteen Psalms of Ascent (Psalm 120–134) are filled with great truth worth reflecting on, and they are familiar to most Bible students. Today, we are going to look at fifteen passages from these psalms that are great reminders and are worthy of our attention or our study.

Psalm 120:1: "In my trouble I cried to the Lord, and He answered me."

All of us have times of trouble. In fact, Jesus said, "In this world you will have trouble." Isn't it comforting to know that when we do, our Lord is not only aware, but when we cry out to Him, He will hear and answer. Now, what is that situation or who is that person who creates much trouble for you? As you come into the Lord's presence, hand over the need to Him.

Psalm 121:2: "My help comes from the Lord, who made the heavens and earth."

Are there times when your trials or difficulties seem so insignificant that surely God isn't interested? Or they appear to us so massive that there's no need for us to pray? Here, the psalmist reminds us, if God can create out of nothing all that there is, He can handle your situation. In fact, Psalm 121 reminds us that the Creator is our helper, keeper, and protector; He will never fall asleep on the job. Now, think about that.

Psalm 121:7: "The Lord will protect you from all evil; He will keep your soul."

Have you ever stopped to think how many sicknesses, wrecks, catastrophes, or near-misses you have been protected from? A few years ago, I was coming out of the woods after a morning of unsuccessfully seeking Bambi's dad. I had taken Clay, our youth pastor, over to my brother's land to hunt. As we were unloading our rifles to prepare to leave, Clay's rifle malfunctioned and shot into the ground, right between my legs. Needless to say, if the gun has been aimed a few inches to the left or right, my leg would have been blown off, and I probably wouldn't be here to write about this; the Lord is our protector. And if you do lose your life in some unfortunate situation, He will keep your soul.

Psalm 122:1: "I was glad when they said to me, let us go to the house of the Lord."

Reader, can I help you with something? It's not that we *have* to go to church; we *get* to. Time in God's house with God's people, hearing God's Word and singing God's praises, should make our heart glad. If that's not the case, you better examine your heart or consider another church.

Psalm 122:6: "Pray for the peace of Jerusalem: may they prosper who love you."

Jerusalem, or Mount Zion, is unlike any other place in the world, and it is one of the few places in scripture we are specifically told to pray for. Every believer should love the Holy Land and should regularly pray for the peace of Jerusalem. In fact, God promises to bless those who do.

Psalm 123:1: "I will lift up my eyes, O you who are enthroned in the heavens."

The writer looks beyond the palace and porticos of Jerusalem, and his eyes glance towards the heavens, where God is on His throne. Not only does He rule, He overrules. Your circumstances may appear dark and difficult, but God is on His throne, and He sees no emergency in your situation.

Psalm 124:8: "Our help is in the name of the Lord."

A study of the names of God and their meaning is worthwhile. In fact, do a search for His covenant names. Look at the differences in the words "God," "Lord," "Christ," "Messiah," and "Jesus." There is no other name like His. In fact, Acts 4:12 says it clearly: "And there is salvation in no one else; for there is no other name under heaven that has been given among men by which we must be saved."

Psalm 125:1–2: "Those who trust in the Lord are as Mount Zion, which cannot be moved but abides forever ... so the Lord surrounds His people."

Those verses speak to me of a strength and a stability for those who place their faith in the Lord, who trust in Him. Why? Because God surrounds His possession and keeps a watchful eye on His own.

Psalm 126:3: "The Lord has done great things for us; we are glad."

I've often remarked to my family that the best indicator of future outcomes is to look at past events. This is also true in our journey with the Lord. If you want to know how He will act the next time, look back on how He responded the last time. When you have a past with the Lord, it is so much easier to give Him your present and your future.

Psalm 127:1: "Unless the Lord builds the house, they labor in vain who build it."

Michelle and I were praying last night together for many needs and issues. Always at the top of our list is our family; our children, grandchildren, each other, and others. All families have issues and needs. I hear people today talk about coming from a dysfunctional family; eh, don't we all? Here the psalmist mentions children (127:3–5, 128:3b), your wife (128:3a), the man (128:4), grandchildren (128:6), and to sum it up, he writes, "Blessed be everyone that fears the Lord" (128:1). All of our families need the Lord to be our builder and the basis of our faith.

Psalm 129:5: "May all who hate Zion be put to shame and turned backward."

God's chosen land and people have a history filled with opponents, enemies, and adversaries. Many times, Israel has been attacked, and many times, the Jewish people have been persecuted. Still, God came to their rescue and was their defense. In the end, all who oppose God and His people will "wither like the grass" (v. 6). It's always wise to be on the same team as God.

Psalm 130:4: "But there is forgiveness with you, that you may be feared."

The forgiveness of God is an amazing thing. When we confess, God forgives us; it doesn't matter how big our sin is, or how many we commit. I love how Psalm 130 ends. God gives us something to look for (hope), live for (loving kindness), thank the Lord for (redemption), and rejoice in (forgiveness).

Psalm 132:10: "For the sake of David your servant, do not turn away the face of your anointed."

Undoubtedly, Psalm 132 was penned by Solomon, Hezekiah, or someone other than David. The writer seems to imply, "If you won't do this for me, do it because of David." Do you remember the time David blessed Mephibosheth for Jonathon's sake? David didn't even know Mephibosheth, but he blessed him anyway; God blesses us at times not because we deserve it but because Jesus deserves it, and we're in Him.

Psalm 132:13: "For the Lord has chosen Zion; He desired it for His habitation."

Think of that; of all the beautiful and amazing places in the world, when it came time for God to choose His land and His home, He chose

Zion. This location is desired (13), will have rest (14), will be blessed (15), will satisfy (15b), and will be a center of worship (16–17); in the end, Jesus will reign as King. The last time He came, He wore a crown of thorns, but next time, His crown will "shine" (18).

Psalm 134:1–2: "Behold, bless the Lord, all servants of the Lord, who serve by night in the house of the Lord. Lift up your hands in the sanctuary and bless the Lord."

The writer closes out by reminding us that this God we know is worthy of our service and our worship. So lift up your hands and your voices, and praise the One Who is worthy.

I hope you'll go back and read through all of the Psalms of Ascent slowly, in a meditating way; let these truths sink deep into your soul. The next time you feel down and discouraged and ready to quit, don't give up. Go up! As you ascend into the Lord's presence, remember these psalms and these truths. They've gotten Israel through a lot, and they will you as well.

We're marching to Zion
Beautiful, beautiful Zion.
We're marching upward to Zion
The beautiful city of God.

Exploration Guide

1. There are many songs written about Zion and Jerusalem. What are some of your favorites?
2. Discuss the role of Zion in the three areas mentioned in this chapter.

3. Which of the Psalms of Ascent is your favorite and why?

4. Why do you think we are told to pray for the peace of Jerusalem (122:6) and not other locations?

5. Psalm 124:8 says, "Our help is in the name of the Lord." Which of our Lord's names are most dear to you and why?

6. Which has been your most interesting mountain and valley to study and why?

Conclusion

For the last thirty days, it has been a joy to guide you through the land of Israel. We have been from Dan to Beersheba (1 Samuel 3:20), from the Great Sea to the Tigris and Euphrates River Valley. We've gone way up to Mount Hermon and way down to the Dead Sea. Mountains and valleys, highs and lows, peaks and pits.

Really, my purpose in writing this book is threefold. **First**, I wanted you to see the land of our Lord in a fresh and real way. I've grown to love this amazing region and hope you will as well. In fact, I'd love to take you there someday. **Second**, I hope you've come to understand that life too has its mountaintops and its valleys. While writing this book, I've seen this develop personally in our nation. In early 2020, the American economy was blowing it out. Jobs were plentiful, unemployment was low, and people's retirement accounts were swelling. Times were really good.

Then, a strange virus named COVID-19 left Wuhan, China, and began to impact every nation of the world. Due to the negative effects of this unseen enemy, millions of jobs in our country have been lost, 401ks have shrunk, businesses are closing, schools are not meeting, and more than 210,000 Americans will have died, as of this writing. Our great nation was truly riding high, but now, we've been ordered to stay at home. Peak and pits.

What do these times say to us? What do they reveal about us? What is God seeking to do? Here are a few helps for those varying seasons of life, the peaks and pits:

P   Pray much. Don't stop now; you didn't get here on your own.

E   Enjoy your moment of victory, for a downturn may be just ahead.

A   Accept the good (and bad) as part of the Father's plan; He uses both.

K   Keep your eyes firmly fixed on the Lord. "Fixing our eyes on Jesus, the author and perfecter of our faith" (Hebrews 12:2).

S   Store up some of the great truths you learned on the mountains; you'll need those reminders to get you through the valleys.

P   Praise always. "Rejoice in the Lord always" (Philippians 4:4). Paul and Silas leave us a great example in Acts 16. This will help you and confuse the world.

I   Investigate your heart (Psalm 51). We dig many of our own pits; David sure did.

T   Have a thankful spirit. Give thanks for everything, not just the good stuff. When we learn to be thankful for our undesirable situations, we know we've begun to grow.

S   Serve the Lord while in the valley; anybody can do so while on a mountain. God will grow and mature your heart more in times of peril and pain than in sunshine and laughter.

Third, I also wrote this book to tell you I've been on life's mountain, but I've also had my share of valleys. I finally found my life's purpose some four decades ago when I began to understand my sin and God's grace. I came to know Jesus Christ in a personal way, not just a head knowledge but a heart experience. No, I didn't find religion, as many of my peers thought; I now have a personal relationship with the Lord. And I'm here to tell you, that should keep you humble on the mountains and focused in the valleys.

Peaks and pits: I've experienced and *needed* both. You do as well. Amen.

Soli Deo Gloria.

Let's Get Together

Now that you've finished *Peaks and Pits,* you may want to read my two previous books, *Big Doors Swing on Small Hinges* (2014) and *Sail On ... Examining the Ships of the Bible* (2016). I would love to hear from you and get your thoughts on my books or just discuss this thing we call life. If my books have been an encouragement to you, I hope you'll consider sharing them with others.

I hope you'll visit my website rogermardis.com and friend me or follow me on Facebook, Twitter, and Instagram.

Also, I'm available to visit your church, small group, missions conference, or event. You can get in touch with me through any of my social media accounts or by email roger@friendsofnazareth.org, or you can drop by our office located at 219 Simpson Street, Florence, Alabama, 35630.

Remember, we endure the pits so we can enjoy the peaks. Blessings.

Dr. Roger D. Mardis, President
Friends of Nazareth

What Makes the Friends of Nazareth (FON) Ministry Unique?

FON is the only 501 (c) (3) corporation dedicated to providing ministry/financial support to Nazareth Baptist School. Note: Since 1991, NBS has not received funds from the Southern Baptist Cooperative Program. At that time, NBS became a private Evangelical Christian school recognized by the Israeli Ministry of Education, and it remains such.

No other organization is dedicated and committed to **helping NBS enrich and enlarge its capacity for ministry as well as improve and relocate its school plant**. FON operates through partnerships with churches, Christian schools, and individuals who help it enrich and enlarge the school's evangelism and discipleship programs.

What Makes NBS Unique?

NBS is peerless. It stands alone among the forty-eight Christian schools in Israel. It is the **only K–12th Christian school in Israel that**

1. is Baptist as well as Evangelical,
2. is recognized by the Israeli Ministry of Education,
3. mandates **Bible study and age-graded chapel attendance**,
4. sponsors Evangelistic programs, such as summer camps, sports programs/camps, music camps, and arts camps. **FON/NBS**

camps are endorsed by the **Ministry of Education due to their quality and value-based teaching,**

5. has a biblically based Leadership Development Program for its staff,

6. is a partner with **Student Leadership University,** Dr. Jay Strack, CEO, and

7. offers **cross-cultural school partnerships.** Students have short-term study tours in the USA and US partner schools have short-term study tours in Nazareth.

What Makes a FON Donor Unique?

FON donors are the primary financial resource for ministry with NBS in the hometown of Jesus. FON works in tandem with NBS to coordinate partnership opportunities that fulfill the vision of **building the rising generations and glorifying Jesus Christ through distinctive education.** FON has on-the-ground personnel as well as a partnership with the IMB.

Friends of Nazareth
219 Simpson Street
Florence, Alabama 35630
info@friendsofnazareth.org

A higher standard.
A higher purpose.